CONTEN

PREFACE

William Fisher's three letters describing the Senghenydd mining disaster of 1913 and the Diary of the First World War were shown to me in 1992 by his son Sydney, the "young, uncompromising rebel of two years" of the letters. I was enormously impressed, both by the content of the work and the standard of the writing.

William was my father's younger brother. There appears to have been a family rift because I grew up believing I had no relatives apart from my parents, my brother and my sisters. Recent research into the family background has revealed a fascinating picture of the life and times of an impressive family.

Charles Fisher, a stonemason, had one daughter and three sons - Charles (my father), William (of the diary), and George. My grandmother died when George was born and the children were split up amongst various relatives. My grandfather moved to Cheltenham and became the first Labour candidate for that very Conservative borough. He was an ardent believer in the efficacy of education and served on various committees to further his aims. His speeches recorded in the local papers at the time prove how far in advance of his time he was.

Will became a coalminer, working in many of the South Wales pits. His experiences at Senghenydd when he helped in the rescue operations affected him deeply, as the three surviving letters show. His work there also had a more sinister effect, in that it was the start of the TB which eventually killed him. When the First World War broke out he went to enlist; his wife made no demur because she assumed he would not, with TB, be accepted. But he concealed his state of health and then spent the next four years in the Royal Engineers -and wrote the diary.

There seems little doubt that Will was an aggressive agnostic who took a real delight in fiery arguments with clergymen – and others – who disagreed with him. For me the most interesting fact is that such a man should have taken pride, at the end of his service life, in having worked his way up through the various ranks and always achieved the higher grade by merit. He surely could not have approved of the authorities and what was being done – but he conformed and accepted the discipline. I suspect that few men in his position would do the same today.

In recent research into family history I have heard many stories of Will that may merit a full biography. His son, though he was young when Will died, has many vivid memories of him, most importantly being woken up in the middle of the night and taken out to look at the stars – and listen to a dissertation on the constellations. Unfortunately Sydney was rather afraid of his father – he felt he had a lot to live up to! But he does know that he was an outstanding man.

Just before he died in 1922 Will was visited by his nephew, Charles Knight, and asked the boy if he had any literary aspirations. Charles said he had. Will said, "Well, get down to it; you'll have to make up for all the things I won't have time to write now." I like to think that he, who wanted to write and had so little time for it, should appear in print at last. The original diary, handwritten in a battered little notebook which went all the way through the war with him, is still in the possession of his son. It is this son, Sydney Fisher, who has authorised the present publication.

Elaine H. Fisher
Monmouth, 1997

THE SENGHENYDD LETTERS

Historical Context

On 14 October 1913 one of the worst disasters in British mining history occurred. There was an explosion at Senghenydd in the heart of the South Wales coalfield and 900 men were trapped underground. They were imprisoned behind a wall of fire, their supply of good air cut off. The total death toll was 439.

Will Fisher had just come off shift when the explosion took place. He immediately went underground again to help with the rescue operations. The following three letters describe his experiences – and emotions – there; and the effect the appalling conditions had on his own health.

Letter from Will Fisher to his cousin,
Charlie Mason

Twyn Cottages
Beddau
Caerphilly
Glam.

Wednesday, November 11th, 1913.

Dear Charlie,

Your letter of the 8th to hand.

A month has gone since this terrible calamity
occurred; we have recovered 165 bodies so far; and
280 still remain below in that deadly atmosphere.
Every possible difficulty faces us; roads blocked here
and there by falls of roof, ventilation doors blown
down, thus disorganizing ventilation altogether; con-
sequently mining experts from all over the country
are here devising ways and means of carrying ventilation in small sections by erecting brattice sheets
here, and doors there, to enable us to penetrate the
workings and snatch away the bodies.

Four shifts of six hours each continually keep the
work going. We follow the air current, level down
falls, erect temporary timber making it safe to travel,
then carry away the bodies. At times the gas
(carbon monoxide) beats us, and we have to clear out
for a shift or two, retiring towards pit bottom,
repairing and opening out the mains till the ventilation
is right again.

Three weeks ago we entered Kimberley Dist *(rict)*,
worked our way along a mile and half of main road,
but failed to reach to coal faces where most of the
men are employed; we passed numbers of bodies on
the way (traffic men), lying all shapes; faces
downwards on the road, or sitting on the roadside, a
haulier blown under his tram, the horse lying across
the tram, one man buried by a fall, his foot sticking

2

out; another caught by the full blast, dismembered, his head yards away; a haulage engineman sitting behind his brakes, huddled up, his head sunk on his breast. All killed instantly.

Some of us were levelling falls, just making a small passage for people to travel over. After some two hours my mate complained of feeling unwell and I felt a severe headache coming on, and a sensation akin to alcoholic intoxication creeping over me; the after-damp was on us. So we sat on the roadside; after a while the advance party came staggering back: "Try and get out, boys." And what a job we had; struggling on a few yards, then resting; the stronger helping the weaker.

Were it not for the rescue brigade with their oxygen apparatus, who came in after us, we would never have got out alive; am enclosing a press cutting. I have always had a craze for new experiences; of late I've been busy with them. This is the third time I have faced death; but this time there was no excitement; my brain was more or less active, and my interest in unusual phenomena was aroused. How would these men I knew so well act under the circumstances? It was a verification of our determinist position that man is good by nature. No-one failed in his duty. I noticed no individual scramble for himself. All or none must be saved.

It was a week after this before we could enter this Dist *(rict)* again. We fetched the bodies off the main road, but failed to reach the faces and the colliers remain there yet.

Last week we managed to explore one of the four districts, Ladysmith, on the new plan of ventilating a small section, exploring it, then letting it fill with gas again; shifting the air current on to another section. We cleared the whole district of bodies, with the exception of five, who must be buried under the large falls which will be cleared later. We locate the bodies

3

under the smaller falls by the stench, digging them
out (a horrible job), but the big falls bury them too
deep – that is a titbit for a future occasion.

There is one high fall along Ladysmith Main, a
hundred yards long and forty feet high in one place;
that means at least 1,000 tons to be filled away.

In one 'heading' we found twelve men in a group;
they had missed the blast, had gathered together, and
been killed by afterdamp (carbon monoxide). And
what a spectacle! A dead horse lay rotting near by,
and the men had fallen all shapes: some had sat and
died in a heap. some stretched on their backs, six
were lying across one another; mortification had
played havoc, faces and bare arms white with mildew.
The nauseating stench added to the horror of it all.
In other places the poor fellows had been killed
(?) mercifully at work, stooping cutting coal, their
tools fallen by them. One on the 'main' had his
clothes burnt right off him. One man was on his
knee by a full tram of coal, chalking his number. The
blast in one place had blown a horse and tram against
the coal face, pinning a father and son against the
coal. A sickening sight. The awful tragedy of it all;
the criminal negligence involved. And the 'Coal Mines
Regulation Acts' were passed in 1872, forty years
ago, and amended times since; and these preventable
holocausts still occur.

> The stooped urn, filling, dips and flashes;
> The bronzed brims are deep in ashes;
> The pale old lips of Death are fed;
> Shall this dust gather flesh hereafter?
> Shall one shed tears, or fall to laughter,
> At sight of all these poor old dead?"
> *(A.C. Swinburne, "Ilicet", 1866)*

Then the 'Dead March', what a nightmare. We draw
on leather gloves, lift a body onto a sheet of brattice
cloth, wrap it up, then tie it on a stretcher. "Off

with it, boys", and what a journey, even to us, used to pit work. Through the murky gloom, dimly lit by the swinging lamps carried by the bearers, broken timbers overhead, cracking with the continual squeeze; stumbling over the rough road with the swaying burdens, slipping on rails, sleepers, rough stones, stepping over small falls; timber, here and there the carcase of a horse stretched across the road, burst and mortifying. Climbing big falls, squeezing through small, hastily prepared passages, great stones hanging overhead, likely to fall any minute. One did fall and broke a stretcher. And the stupefying heat and bad air, causing the sweat to pour down one in streams, and to add to the romance the sickening stench, rising all the time to the face of the man behind. In one place, wading to our knees in water, one man fell with the stretcher. Some bodies are heavy too, our wrists giving out before the two miles are covered. Now the pit bottom is reached and the cold air chills to the bone. In the carriage with the burden; the hitcher presses the button, up we go, half a mile of shaft in less than a minute, a rushing and settling. Then across the colliery yard, lit by electricity, through groups of men and women, "Who is it?" "Don't know, indeed", on we go. To the mortuary, walls piled with coffins; men come forward, noses and mouths covered; unwrap the body, calling out to a man with a book, "Moleskin trousers, patch on left knee, nailed boots, piece on right heel", etc., etc., usually the only means of identification, as faces are unrecognizable. Twenty have so far been buried unidentified, owing to melting. Funerals take place every day, the sad processions slowly winding their way to the hillside cemetery.

The pity of it all, that flesh should be so cheap!

The 20th century, the age of luxury! The triumph of wealth production! of labour-saving and life-saving appliances! And 450 of the highest evolved species of animal needlessly sacrificed!!

Everyone in connection with mining, and anyone outside who reads at all, knows that accumulations of gas
can be prevented by efficient ventilation; that dusty
roads can be avoided by regular waterings. Why the
hell are these things neglected? Because of the
expense! And labour being so dirt-cheap, look you!
the average L.W. *(? colliery company)* turns over its
invested capital every eight years; and the
capitalists' bloodstained claw still reaches for more.

I don't expect the manager of the colliery, the mines
agent for the district, together with the managing
director of the colliery company, Lord Merthyr, will
be arraigned for manslaughter; but suffering Christ,
they should be! I don't know if I shall stay through
the exploring. I am fed up. Emily, always prejudiced
against pit-work, is ten times so now. I like this
locality, too. We live in a beautifully wooded district,
just outside the old town of Caerphilly, four miles
from Senghenydd, training to work, nights 9 - 3. I
walk back, down a lovely valley. I have been fairly
well satisfied here too; £2.1.0 for a 48-hour week,
and not too much work. From our doorstep we can
see fields and lanes and woods, and little solitary
dingles running between the mountains. Such walks,
such a wealth of treasure to a nature-lover. The days
this grand summer that I have lain with a book in the
shadow of the old mediaeval castle. Yes, I like this
place better than any before.

Am pleased to hear of the success of the M.E. Union;
all industries are grouping now, and labour is
beginning to understand. Look at New Zealand. The
Enginemen's, Stokers' and Surface Craftsmen's Union
has decided to merge with the S*(outh)* W*(ales)* Miners'
Federation. Of course the capitalist octopus is not
afraid of petty little Labour MPs but it shudders at
the 'New Labour Movement'.

We four are well; the baby, Syd, is a young, uncompromising rebel of two years; the girl, Kate, a little
philosopher of three and a half. I trust you and

yours are well. If I come to Birmingham at Christmas, or before, I will let you know.

I remain your sincere cousin

(Signed) Will Fisher

Letter from Will Fisher to his cousin, Charlie Mason

33 St. Cenydd Terrace
Penyrheol
Caerphilly
Glam.

Tuesday, March 3rd, 1914

Dear Charlie,

I believe it is your turn to write; but as I have got something of interest to write about, and plenty of spare time on my hands, I thought I would write out of my turn; if only for a pastime. I wrote of a great tragedy; well, as far as my little world is concerned, this is a tragedy.

The fact is I have given up work for this last three weeks, failed for the first time in my life, and the cause is pulmonary tuberculosis!! Quite a surprise packet, isn't it? I believe my vitality was lowered during that terrible exploring work at Senghenydd; but the work was dangerous, unusual and thrilling. What with no air, poor air, poisonous gases; extreme heat, then extreme cold at pit bottom, taking our bodies up; working on some jobs, making air-ways over falls, working ten minutes at a spell, heroes all? But damn fools in the bargain. Wading through water up to our knees, then walk home four miles. Well, just after I started at Llanbradach, a hot pit, I started a cough, not an unusual winter visitor. But other winters I shake them off in a few weeks; this bugger is with me now and has made place for another fellow.

Three weeks ago a pain in my right lung stopped me working. The doctor didn't like the sound of my lung and was afraid it was affected. Last Saturday I was sent to a tuberculosis doctor, who put me through it; sent my spittle off to Brompton F. *(?)* Hospital, London, gave me a form of application to the Glamorgan Insurance Company for sanatorium treatment; and there the story remains, to be continued in our next. No-one knows, of course, how things will turn, of course, with the exception of Him "Who threw us down in the field".

If I get away early I ought to pull through; but in any case I shall sample a few more "new experiences" – my hobby! It's finished for a time; grinding out blood- and sweat-stained dividends. And the titbit of the lot, Charlie, if I go, I have to be converted! All dying atheists are converted, as you are aware. I can just imagine the crows coming sniffing around. I would see they get invited. I've often smacked my lips years ago at the thought of a job like that.

Looking at it from a philosophic point of view, death should have no terrors for a wage-slave, especially one who is as acutely conscious of the colossal crime of capitalism as I am.

I fight to live, to live to fight, as a moral duty; but if the Reaper overtakes me, well, I am confident of the little I lose by going.

Well, it is getting late, I must to bed. I feel first-class all day; except for the cough, troubles me mostly night and morning; it pulls me about a bit too.

Sorry to burden you with such an unpleasant subject but it happens to be my present subject of interest and our natures crave for variety.

Remember me to your wife; trust she and family are well. Remember me also to your mother, brothers and sisters.

I remain your sincere cousin.

(Signed) Will Fisher

Letter from Will Fisher to his cousin, Charlie Mason

33 St. Cenydd Terrace
Penyrheol
Caerphilly
Glam.

Monday, 30 March 1914

Dear Charlie,

In answer to yours of the 7th, accept my con-gratulations at your appointment in the MEA *(Midlands Electricity Authority?);* 'tis a fine scope for your energies. What has become of the Gas-workers' Union? You people seem to have cut them out. What are you doing at the Power Station now? Still carpenter and handyman generally?

I believe I explained in my last how this disease of mine originated. A cough contracted just after the Senghenydd exploring work, but I took no particular notice of it, being used to this winter visitor. A touch of pleurisy six weeks ago caused me to have an examination, which revealed the flaw in my lung. Since then I have been idle. I was sent to the tuberculosis doctor - we have a number of them in South Wales. They are in direct touch with the Glamorgan Insurance Committee. He declared I was

9

not fit for sanatorium treatment, my temperature being too high, ordered me to bed until it became normal. I was put on domiciliary treatment. This is the fourth week I am in bed: twice I have got up, but my temperature has gone up again. And back I have had to come. I know a young woman whom it took twelve weeks' bed to fetch down. I am not bad, I don't dislike this at all, I read and sleep all day. But the doctor says encouragingly that I am dying while my temperature stays up.

Saturday He says he is ordering me away to Cardiff Hospital at once; from there when fit I shall go on to the sanatorium. This is luck, as there were 196 applications for sanatorium treatment in the last six weeks; reported at last meeting Glamorgan Insurance Committee. This is an interesting (if a wicked) old world. I don't think I'll leave it yet awhile.

Remember me to Lizzie and the rest of your family. We are still four in family. How many are you?

Father was here last Saturday.

Your sincere cousin.

(Signed) Will Fisher

THE ARMY DIARIES

Historical Context

When the First World War broke out in August 1914 Will Fisher was ill with tuberculosis. With his acknowledged love of new sensations, he was determined to try "soldiering on active service" *(See diary entry for 23.9.15)*. By January 1915 he managed to get into the Royal Engineers by concealing his medical record.

His diary was kept with scrupulous care throughout and the original is still in existence. A transcript follows, together with his book list. An avid reader, he also kept his own handwritten book of favourite quotations and this has survived, together with what is almost certainly his own copy of *Omar Khayyam*; the latter has passed to the present editor via her father, Will's brother Charles.

The Army Diaries

March 1915 - June 1919

The original is a ruled hard-covered notebook, four inches by six, bound at the top, containing 80 sheets. The inside front cover bears the following notes:

Sapper William Fisher No.7349 R A Royal Engineers

Birmingham January 23 1915

Lance-Corporal	1.11.1915	**(11 November in orders)**
Second Corporal	1.12.1915	**(18 December In orders)**
Corporal	1.1.1916	
Sergeant	18.3.1917	
Company Sgt.Major	2.5.1919	

Friday, 5 March
Pay four shillings.

Sunday, 7 March
Range.

Monday, 8 March
With Armourers, marking rifles.

Tuesday, 9 March
Had new teeth with dentist.

Friday, 12 March
Pay five shillings.

Sunday, 14 March
Range. On the cliffs facing Irish Sea, watching for passing ships.

Monday, 15 March
Put on Musketry.
Started the mile run before break!

Friday, 19 March
Pay four shillings.

Saturday, 20 March
Trade Test, passed as Walling Mason one and fourpence rate with one and tuppence = half a crown a day.

Sunday, 21 March
Musketry practice.

Friday, 26 March
Pay five shillings. Name down for next draft.

Sunday, 28 March
Divine Service

Monday, Tuesday, Wednesday, 29, 30, 31 March
Miniature Rifle Range. Did first class.

Good Friday, 2 April
Big Range firing. Pay four shillings.

Saturday, 3 April
Range. Rain soaked to skin.
No leave granted.

Monday, 5 April
Drilling on sea front.

Wednesday, 7 April
Firing on Range – Second highest of party of 40.

Thursday, 8 April
Started course of Field Works, Bridge Building, etc.

Thursday, 15 April
Away to Caernarvon for 9 days; fixing barbed wire around Marconi Station; living in blockhouse. Slight haemorrhage.

Saturday, 24 April
Returned to Kingswood Camp.

Sunday, 25 April
Final medical inspection – passed for foreign service. Home for 5 days. Free railway pass. Drew £5, including trade pay.

Friday, 30 April
Returned. Detonators, demolitions, explosives. Told to prepare to be sent any moment across the seas. Trench digging. Learning trench warfare. Nights.

Sunday, 9 May
Served out with equipment, routemarching with it up.

Thursday, 13 May
Left Anglesey for France. Draft of 60. Pay ten shillings. Trained at Bangor 9.0 p.m.

Friday, 14 May

Reached Southampton 3.0 p.m.. Embarked 7.30 p.m. on troop ship with RAMC, ASC and Dispatch Riders, also DCLI, about 800 of us. Lovely weather, felt first class. Transport attended by two destroyers.

Saturday, 15 May

Up River Seine to Rouen. Grand old French city. Notre Dame. Lovely river the Seine, lined with woods, small towns and villages. Base of British Expeditionary Force four miles outside Rouen. This base a high affair; men passing on and men returning wounded.

Sunday, 16 May

Off to the front. We are here waiting at a large station in Rouen, in an extensive refreshment room. Troops of all sorts (dragoons, Army Medical Corps, engineers, artillery) are here, drinking, feeding, singing, dancing. All are brimming over with good health and spirits. Yet thousands of men in the base returning from the war zone tell bloodcurdling tales of the horrors of modern warfare. Our little draft are going up to make up a company who have been badly cut up in a recent engagement.

Monday, 17 May

Arrived at Hazebrouck within sound of the big guns. Slept in train Sunday night. Can't go further yet, await orders. Sleep in goods shed at night to go on in the morning.

Tuesday, 18 May

Trained to Poperinge and over Belgian frontier. Marched on to Ypres. Joined Holyhead siege company RA RE, living in dugouts. One blanket, mud, mud.

Wednesday, 19 May

Making dugouts, fetching old timber from the deserted city of Ypres. Roofs and walls

perforated, household goods left. Piles of
material wealth everywhere. Cathedral, Cloth
Hall, large asylum wrecked.

Thursday, 20 May

Making reserve line of trenches other bank of
Yser Canal; canal bank all honeycombed with
dugouts with troops. Two miles from advanced
trenches; all around here scattered batteries of
guns, concealed, booming day and night. German
guns shelling here, making holes one could bury
horse and cart. Two German aeroplanes over
here all afternoon trying to locate our guns. Our
aerial guns firing shrapnel at them. Saw one hit,
which fell inside our line.

Friday, 21 May

Digging trenches. Big gun fixed handy dugout,
discharge shakes us. G *(erman)* aero *(plane)* above
all evening – we fail to drop it.

Sunday, 23 May

Trenches. Two of our chaps wounded with
shrapnel, five enemy aircraft overhead, seem to
have located batteries, shells dropping all around
here, number of casualties; turned in
apprehensive.

Whit Monday, 24 May

Terrific bombardment. Turned out at 3.0 a.m.,
choking with gas, had to wear respirators. A
hasty scramble, deafening roar and crash of shellfire. On way to work noted effect of night's
bombardment. Houses smashed, roads torn up,
wounded men returning from trenches, Red Cross
vans with men choking with bromine gas. Five
horses killed with battery next field to us. While
at work having to shelter down in trench as
shrapnel burst near us. Fortunately one hears
the shells approach. A big shell dropped in our
open air cookhouse; cooks hopped it in time.
Shell burst amongst our chaps today, killed four,
wounded three. Only a leg remained of one.

Twelve out of fifteen guns around here put out of
action in 24 hours and 130 casualties. Terrible
day's fighting. Germans using gas shells. Men
everywhere choking or wounded.

Friday, 28 May
Pay four and tuppence.

Sunday, 30 May
On 24 hours guard, two on, four off; convenient
to get washing done. Two of our chaps got three
months for being absent and drunk four hours,
put down as deserters.

Friday, 4 June
Another chap injured, hand smashed. Shrapnel
burst over our heads.

Sunday, 6 June
Making new dugouts. Moved to them about a
mile. Still near batteries; shells flying around.

Monday, 7 June
Still working beside Yser Canal; trenches,
dugouts, etc. One of our chaps found drunk –
14 days, five-shilling fine.

Thursday, 10 June
First wet day, drenched to the skin. A chap who
referred to this in letter home was tried for 'false
accusation against officer'. Seven days 'field
punishment', tied to cart, etc.

Sunday, 13 June
Finished on canal side. Sgt.Major Mignett takes
charge of company.

Tuesday, 15 June
Clearing Grand Place, Ypres, of fallen masonry
for passage of troops. Cloth Hall and St.
Martin's Cathedral beautiful old specimens of
architecture. The Germans shelled us from there;
lucky to get away without casualties.

Wednesday, 16 June

Big battle in progress. Our sections relieving one another in keeping roads clear, shell-holes filled, etc. Shells bursting all around, streams of wounded straggling past us, bloodstained and weary. Beautiful day! Sgt.Major passed, wrist broken, carrying German helmet. On 6 - 10 then 10 - 2 night. Hooge, three lines of trenches taken. Roads choked with supply wagons, Red Cross vans. Men being relieved from the trenches, weary and mudstained. Groups of German prisoners passing, average a sturdy lot, well fed. Our New Army of poor physical appearance with exception of Highland Regiments. All report taking of German trenches but evening sees no diminution of shellfire. Nine aeroplanes soaring above us. Observation balloons still up. Number of RGA men wounded near us.

Thursday, 17 June

Parcel and five shillings from Emm. [*His wife Emily; her brother, Private George Branaghan of the 1st Worcs. Regiment, killed at Neuve Chapelle.*] News that brother-in-law George is killed. Working in sections, six-hour days, still clearing Ypres. Houses falling in, filled with expensive furniture and wealth of every description, fast going to ruin. Looting difficult to check, penalties severe. Military police constantly making arrests.

Friday, 18 June

Still clearing roads in Ypres.

Saturday, 19 June

Fresh job repairing reserve trenches - plenty of shells dropping near us. Night on road patrol duty in Ypres, thirteen hours. Refreshed ourselves from wine cellar, ruined house. Fine night. About midnight Gordon Highlanders returning from 26 days in the trenches. Each company passing with its pipers playing. Quite a nice effect: the weird but stirring music of the pipes and the regular if slow beat of the marching troops on the cobbled roadway; the gradual dying away of the music in the distance and only the occasional bursting of a shell and the distant volleying of rifle fire in the trenches disturbing the silence of the night.

Sunday, 20 June
Well-earned day off. Slept like the dead. Afternoon bath and change. Then lounge with an old paper. We are not allowed to leave camp.

Friday, 25 June
Raining, and we are sheltering in dugouts in the trenches we are repairing. Been out six weeks now under shellfire more or less the whole time; to work every day, there is nothing to distinguish one day from another. Up at 6, start away 8, return at 5, turn in 9. Confined to camp every evening – just lounge and read. Change of locality and work the only matters of interest. But summing it up I would as soon be here (for the summer at least) as working in civilian life. The remuneration is very fair comparatively. Wife's allowance 23 shillings; my pay 14 shillings weekly; that is 37 shillings and food and clothes. Would not mind this lasting another three months.

Monday, 28 June
Making big gun foundations; collecting girders from ruined r(ailway) station at Ypres; fine gorge of fruit (red, white and black currants) from deserted gardens.

Tuesday, 29 June
Our Section Officer wounded, shrapnel wound, back of neck. Worked 'til dinner; then word came to knock off; had afternoon free. On night-shift 8 – 3.30, heavy storm, unloading and carrying girders, planks, etc., for gun platforms, troops passing all night, fresh men going up to relieve the others. We are about two miles from

advanced trenches; this is a loop in the line, a
half circle of star-lights indicates the position and
distance, an occasional rifle bullet sings past us as
we work. All around here are concealed
batteries, now and then one hears an order given
and a gun speaks. In the early night German
shrapnel burst over the KRRs as they marched by
us, and a number were wounded and carried to a
handy dressing station; from there ambulance
motors carry them back to the ambulance field
hospitals.

Thursday, 1 July

Men coming from trenches suffering from effects
of gas; told us several had died from it up
there. One gets used to working at night without
light, even building with sandbags; the glow
from the distant trench star-lights at regular
intervals renders assistance.

Saturday, 3 July

Worked all Friday night and this afternoon 2 'til
8. Germans were shelling village in front of us,
buildings were falling and clouds of brickdust
rising at each shot. What few civilians there
were there, and troops, scrambled away in some
haste.

Sunday, 4 July

Quiet day, rest up; some lounging in the sun, a
party sits in the shade at Nap! A number are
stripped, washing by the stream, and others are
washing underclothes. This afternoon a chaplain
visits us and is holding service in the camp. I
am excused. Hymns of praise are going up now
to the God of Battles and Prince of Peace; shells
are falling a couple of fields away. The people of
Christian Europe are at war, animated with the
most primitive of human passions; this after
2,000 years of Christ's teaching, 'Love your
enemies', and yet this damned farce is kept up.
Service is ended now and the chaplain is having
tea with our officers; chairs and table, etc.,

being the result of LOOT. We are often
reminded of the serious nature of looting.

Wednesday, 7 July

Finished gun emplacements. In addition to
girders and timber, each took over 1,400
sandbags to build side walls.

Thursday, 8 July

Repairing trenches. From the high canal path we
can see the firing line, Hill 60 and the Hill of
Death. Were shelled from there in the afternoon.
Shrapnel burst over us but we missed it by
sheltering in trench dugouts. I and another were
caught in a shower of shrapnel, bullets and shell
splinters from first shell.

Friday, 9 July

Off sick, diarrhoea, day's rest.

Saturday, 10 July

On new line of trenches, repairing. Shell
splinters flying around, as usual.

Thursday, 15 July

News of Katie's serious condition: in hospital
with dislocated hip, awaiting operation; feel cut
up over it. [*His daughter Katharine, then aged
four.*]

Sunday, 18 July

Won 20 francs during the week at Nap and Brag.
This evening divine service, then we gather for a
gamble.

Thursday, 22 July

News that daughter Katie has been under X-rays.
Result – tuberculosis in hip. Result of fall in
school playground. This is a severe blow, as I
prized my children's health.

Saturday, 24 July

Building dugouts against trenches for troops'
winter quarters.

Sunday, 25 July

Rumours of great preparations for a big 'do' here, evidently the long-promised 'Big Advance'. Our batteries increasing all the time here. Very poor weather, stormy and cold nights all the month, very little sunshine seen. German aeroplane brought down in flames. The weekly service a regular thing now.

Thursday, 29 July

New draft of 30 arrived, late at night, with Lieut. Way.

Friday, 30 July

Coming up to the work this morning, we passed scores of our wounded returning from trenches; had been heavy bombardment during the night, Germans have taken trenches of ours. This is dinner-time, there is to be British counter-attack this afternoon; our reinforcements have been pouring up past us all the morning. Had an awful time of it this afternoon. Our job was directly in front of a battery of ours. Bombardment started by us, soon resulting in terrific artillery duel. We were forced to hide under cover. Place was an INFERNO of bursting shells, with the roar of our batteries and the bursting of big coal-boxes, shrapnel, whizz-bangs and the more dangerous silent shells, the latter bursting without warning. The sandbags in our trench were being ripped everywhere by shell splinters; 'twas a marvel we escaped so well. Galbraith and Tully of our section were killed, the latter one of the new draft [*arrived the previous day*]. We escaped more casualties by crawling along the trenches away from the shell-swept area. The Germans took 300 yards of our trenches at Hooge.

Saturday, 31 July

Our section gave Galbraith a military funeral. Fighting going on all day. Lieut.-Col. RE, Brig.-General and a Major RA killed near us. One of our 9.2 inch guns burst at Vlamertinge K <u>6</u> W 8. *(?)*

Sunday, 1 August

Engagement still on. Afternoon off because of bombardment. News that Father is going under operation, am afraid of the consequences, owing to age. [*His father Charles Fisher, a stonemason, was then 66 and survived Will by two years, dying in 1924.*]

Monday, 2 August

Lieut.Way takes over our Section, extremely Regimental, very hard man, had me on the carpet twice in Beaumaris *(Anglesey).*

Wednesday, 4 August

Company taken to Poperinge for bath and clean change. First reg. *(? regular)* bath in seven months. I prefer the open air wash in the camp.

Thursday, 5 August

Intimation that I am in for promotion; this is second time. Troops passing camp shelled 17K 33In. *(?)*

Saturday, 7 August

Another 10 francs pay. Burns of Section 3 wounded in shoulder.

Sunday, 8 August

Been out here 13 weeks. Feel well, health consistent, cough most gone. Twelve months ago in South Devon one hardly thought it possible I should be here this time. If I continue missing the shells, this military service will have been a big advantage from a health point of view.

Monday, 9 August

We retook trenches lost at Hooge and 200 prisoners.

Tuesday, 10 August

Germans tried to retake them, but were beaten off.

Friday, 13 August
Lieut.Way off ill. We have about a third of Company always on sick list.

Saturday, 14 August
Back on trenches right of railway; shelled from there, dugouts we left smashed in, equipment buried.

Tuesday, 17 August
Our work in observation from German lines, shifting job every day, owing to shelling.

Wednesday, 18 August
Camp shelled out, shifted mile back, lying between Dikkebusch and Vlamertinge. Cottage demolished. Day making dugouts and moving in.

Thursday, 19 August
Making 6 ft. drain, heavy job, 3-mile walk to it. Working in six inches of mud.

Monday, 23 August
16 shillings pay.

Tuesday, 24 August
Our Company now attached to 3rd Division taking place of 56th RE (Reg.). We start to go to advanced trenches. Sec. 1 and 3 go up tonight.

Wednesday, 25 August
On guard 24 hours. Lovely day, aeroplanes (G) floated hawklike overhead, 'til chased away by shrapnel from our anti-aircraft guns, visible by bursting puffs of smoke. News of German naval reverse in Baltic. Yesterday the Germans shelled our road to camp as we returned in the evening; had to make a big detour across country with shell splinters flying over us; could see people running frantically from the houses, returning after firing ceased.

Saturday, 28 August

One of our big guns 9.2 burst this evening in a farm, just behind our dugouts, 5 killed, 9 wounded. A new gun, just arrived. 6th shot.

Sunday, 29 August

Rain knocked us off. Wet night, enjoying R. Chambers' *Maids of Paradise,* a fine book. Finished our big drain.

Monday, 30 August

To go to advanced trenches this evening. On fatigues this morning, turfing our dugouts. Tried for transfer to Tunnelling Company RE. Afraid it's a bad egg.

Tuesday, 31 August

Our section went to trenches last night, right into the loop beyond Zillebeke, Chancery Wood *(? Sanctuary Wood)*, making dugouts. Highly dangerous too, the firing trenches running round to right and left of us; stray bullets whistling past us from both sides. Arrived after dark and leaving before dawn; long walk, about six miles from camp, approaching job single file through communication trench, silently moving along passing infantry, bullets hissing over the parapets. Beautiful country up toward the Line, undulating low hills, woods, the scene of scores of battles, through the deserted and battered village of Zillebeke, once so picturesque, with its pretty houses, trees, gardens, fine old church now battered and torn, looking ghastly in the light of the star-shells from the trenches. AND EVERYWHERE CROSSES OF THE MEN WHO FELL. Returned to camp done up; called up to do fatigues so we protested. I was selected to state case to C.O. who met us and agreed to ease things. Stopped fatigues and granted concessions.

Wednesday, 1 September

Last night motor lorry took us couple of miles and met us returning 3.0 a.m., big help too.

Friday, 3 September

Last night finished our job by Chancery Wood; a hell of a night too. On the journey forward took shelter in reserve trenches from German bombardment. Nearby 12 of the 4th Lincolns were killed by shell. Rained all night, worked through to get job done, drenched to the skin, plastered in mud, six inches of mud everywhere. Falling in ditches was common occurrence. Walking was a proper misery. Stayed in bed all day. Rained all the time; night off. Just rose to meals, properly tired out.

Monday, 6 September

Been three days at the ramparts, south-east side of Ypres. Repairing trenches, in charge of a small party of chaps, a CORPORAL'S job. Been out here four months now. The rain these last few days has considerably increased the hardships of campaigning, the trenches being in such a state with mud and water and, to make matters worse, the lack of facilities for drying one's clothes in camp. The dugout roofs let in water too. So far wet feet and damp clothes have not caused any ill effects, but am afraid they will and then undo the good work built up this last eight months.

Tuesday, 7 September

Repairing another section of trenches (HQ), torn about by shellfire. J. Feltham (Sec. 1) killed, shell splinters; Corp.McYouen *(?)* (Sec. 3) injured by fall. Court Martial: Williams 8 weeks, Tarpey 10 weeks, drunk.

Tuesday, 14 September

Had 9 days' glorious sunshine. Off today. Off to the trenches tonight.

Wednesday, 15 September

Last night repairing GH2 Lines. *(? GHQ = General Headquarters)*

Thursday, 16 September

Started building dressing station in Maple Wood,

beyond Zillebeke. A biggish job to hold 50 patients, sandbag walls five feet thick. Working in the dark, just occasional flashes of light from star-shells, bullets whistling through the trees. Long walk through miles of communication trenches; last couple of miles by motor lorry, reaching camp just before dawn. Clear cold nights.

Saturday, 18 September

Severe cold. Took night off. Went to see Dr. Law, a proper blackguard. After exam., declared I was alright and gave me "Duty", equivalent to malingering. So I demanded from SM (*company sergeant-major*) to be charged so as to appeal against medical decision. But I was assured that the medical report was ignored in my case, as my reputation was above that, and was offered another shift off. The humour of it all was that of being declared sound after stethoscope exam. Anyway, the weather is fine and will stick it as long as possible. Am down for promotion. Should like the bars up before going down the line. Because, though I work like steam and keep in good condition, I have no doubt the rains and mud of winter will fetch me down.

Thursday, 23 September

Another evening off; feeling very rough, went sick this evening. Job in Maple Wood nearly finished, was selected to do principal part. No question about advancement if coming season was favourable. Rain beating on dugout, will be coming through tomorrow, I suppose. Just about fed up. May tell doctor about the tuberculosis tomorrow. My cough is gradually coming on again. My faith in a cure is about shattered. But what does it matter after all? This last sensation (soldiering on active service) has worn thin and am getting indifferent about anything and everything. As I write, the ammunition wagons are rumbling past and the music from the bagpipes and kettledrums heralds the return of some regiment of Jocks *(Scottish regiment)* from the trenches.

Friday, 24 September

Reported sick again to Dr. Law, stethoscope exam. – result hospital. Packed my kit, sent to No. 8 Field Ambulance, Brandhoek, kept there all day. Sent on in the evening by ambulance car to No. 10 Casualty Clearing Station, Poperinge. Tremendous general bombardment on, infernal din all night. This day twelve months ago, I left sanatorium; here I am today, the same complaint invaliding me from active service.

Saturday, 25 September

A constant stream of wounded coming in, muddy, bloody and bandaged. Some slightly wounded, exchanging experiences, glad to be on way home; others moaning with pain, carried in on stretchers. Rumours of trenches taken by us, but at tremendous cost. Our trenches ripped to pieces, regiments cut up; machine murder again. Left by ambulance motor for Hazebrouck, Medical Inspection No. 50 Northumbrian CCS, a big reception place, comprising schools and theatre, filled with thousands of sick and wounded lying about on stretchers. Tea served here. Roused up at 10 p.m. Made up a hospital train.

Sunday, 26 September

Train in siding all night. Morning started slowly, away through very fine French country; stranded again at some wayside station; drummed up; biscuits, tin beef, jam, tea. We had 1st-class carriage. Everywhere orchards with ripening fruit. Away again in the evening, none of us knows where, but all hoping it is for across the Channel.

Monday, 27 September

Another night in the train, reaching Le Havre 10 a.m. Station packed with wounded. Medical Officer sorts us out, sick cases waiting aside for convalescent camp. About (?) sick cases put into ambulance cars and taken through Le Havre to Le Havre Convalescent Camp, away on a hillside above the town, a hut camp, a well-built, well-regulated place, good food, reading room. Concerts every evening! The wounded cases sent away by hospital boat to England. Had medical inspection again, steth. exam., no comment, just classified and put away in small canvas huts; everyone speculating as to where we are going. Concert in YMCA Hall; turn in at 9.0 p.m. Not a bad trip altogether, 36 hours in train, two nights and a day, a fine survey of N. France. It appears we were taken to Boulogne, but hospitals full there, then Rouen, same again, so were brought here. A Medical Board sits here every few days; they decide if it is England, hospital out here, or our respective bases again.

Wednesday, 29 September

Still waiting for inspection. Yesterday afternoon concert, first-class artists. This evening lantern lecture, Canada. First-class feeding, best of food.

Thursday, 30 September

On fatigue, laying paving. Men still coming and going. Board of doctors sending about fifth to England.

Saturday, 2 October

Board room; my company being examined. Men in long queue waiting turns; Anxious faces, UP THE LINE or MERRY ENGLAND? Am indifferent myself; am inclined to go back, for various reasons. Exam. by Board, made light of it, thrown to next Board, given cough mixture, no doubt kept back for observation.

Sunday, 3 October

200 of my company left here, hospital ship or

base. On cookhouse fatigues all day. Sacred concert in the evening.

Tuesday, 5 October
Lecture on Napoleon. Professor Patterson.

Wednesday, 6 October
Before Board again, thrown to next Board; chest massage. 300 of us marched through Le Havre to cinema. Concert in evening and address by Chaplain.

Thursday, 7 October
Bulk of the chaps left here now, mostly for the Base. Fatigues every day now. Alwyn huts (canvas) condemned. Marquee tents to replace them. Doctors here very autocratic, patients having no more consideration than cattle. Evening Army Chaplain, lecture on his experiences on the wreck of *Empress of Ireland.* Pay: 10 francs on Tuesday.

Sunday, 10 October
Here two weeks now. Picked up my old form again, clothes getting tight on me, feeding up and manage to dodge fatigues, lounging and reading in YMCA. Concerts or lectures every evening. Ask to return to the Line next Board. Sacred instrumental concert this evening.

Tuesday, 12 October
Afternoon pass into Le Havre.

Wednesday, 13 October
Marched to cinema in the town.

Thursday, 14 October
Medical Board again. Marked Temporary Base, unfit at present. This just suits me, am tired of this place now that I am feeling fit again.

Saturday, 16 October
Left Convalescent Depot for Base.

Sunday, 17 October

Arrived Rouen. Travelled all night by train.
Marched to RE Base Depot. 1,200 here. Drafts
keep coming and going, big numbers of miners'
companies, chemists' companies, lab. and navvies'
companies. The different camps, detail bases,
hospitals, constitute a good-sized town; mostly
bell tents, camps well regulated, up-to-date
sanitation, everyone medically examined before
proceeding up the Line. RE's working every day,
in camp or at Rouen docks. Cookhouse F *(atigue)*
today.

Monday, 18 October

Served out equipment. A rifle to nurse again.

Tuesday, 19 October

F *(atigue)* cutting drains, cinema in evening.

Wednesday, 20 October

Officers' Mess fatigue. Afternoon Medical Board
(three doctors). Col. exam. report, A Service,
quite sound.

Thursday, 21 October

Working at convalescent camp.

Friday, 22 October

Working at horse transport camp.

Saturday, 23 October

Officers' Mess. Pay 15 francs. British miners
coming here; being formed into special companies
and sent up. Met chaps from S *(outh)* Wales I
knew. This base is fairly passable, good food, if
served a bit rough, sleeping in bell tents, a
different job nearly every day. Cinemas and
concerts and lectures. Easy work and good
feeding. Can get into town occasionally.

Sunday, 24 October

Church Parade morning. Football match in camp
afternoon. Down to Rouen evening, big city,

luxuriant cafés, customers playing at dominoes, dice games, etc., ease and comfort. Fine river scene in centre, beats London Victoria Embankment, wide thoroughfares as in Le Havre; English towns cramped as compared to continental. Streets swarmed with stylish girls catering for British Tommies. Camp overlooks city and the Seine valley. Rouen stretches away up valley sides, beautiful country; a day's journey up river from Le Havre, river winding between hills, wooded, with nestling villages. Indian troops hospital next our camp.

Monday, 25 October
Raining; making French scoops *(?)*.

Wednesday, 27 October
Infantry Division Camp: Drain digging.

Thursday, 28 October
Convalescent Camp: On water mains.

Saturday, 30 October
At Cavalry Base. ASC Remount. All crack horse regiments here. Miles of stables, 2,000 horses, fine animals, cost on average £40 apiece.

Monday, 1 November
Go with Terr *(itorial)* RE motor lorry, fetching stores from docks. Rained all day. Gangs of our long–sentence defaulters working as dock labourers. Sergeants in charge, carrying revolvers. Afternoon in Terr. RE Camp Stores. These Terriers have higher standard of living than our Regulars, sleep on beds in canvas huts too.

Tuesday, 2 November
Navvying, Convalescent Camp.

Wednesday, 3 November
Navvying, Terr. Infantry Base.

Thursday, 4 November
Navvying, North Midland Camp.

Friday, 5 November
Rouen docks, concreting engine house. German prisoners working here. ASC Docker Batt., navy-blue uniform, three-shilling-a-day men, unloading, live in huts, go a very easy pace, oldish men. Army Bakery here, big scale, field ovens.

Saturday, 6 November
With motor lorry, fetching timber from the great forest between here and Paris. 20 mile square, all pine trees, grown for commercial purposes, pit props, etc.

Sunday, 7 November
Warned for draft, gambled with cards; evening cinema.

Monday, 8 November
Seven of us and one NCO, ex-hospital cases, start up the Line. Captain RAMC inspected us, telling us if we fail to "carry on" to report to our MO. This is Coffee Room, Rouen Station, as in May when I was here before. Crowds of various British Regiments are entraining for up the Line, fresh uniforms and faces, the same light-heartedness; what a contrast with the crowd I came down with!

Tuesday, 9 November
Trained all last night, this morning through port of Boulogne, pulled up at Calais, made tea and breakfast. Changed Hazebrouck Junction. Reached Poperinge 2.0 p.m. Raining. Marched full marching order to camp; seven miles, properly done up.

Wednesday, 10 November
Rejoined section; making dugout in camp. Conditions improved here, our dugouts re-roofed and stores provided - pair boots.

Thursday, 11 November
Promoted (paid) Lance-Corporal (In Orders).

Friday, 12 November
Raining all day. In dugouts.

Saturday, 13 November
Working on shellproof dugouts for RA Battery.
Corrugated eighth-inch steel arch, 2 ft. concrete,
then cased with sandbags, 2 ft. soft earth, then
sandbags, then soil and turfs = 9 ft.

Sunday, 14 November
Corporal of the Guard, 24 hours. Weather very
cold; one advantage of being NCO, good stove in
Guard Room. Some difficulty in changing then
mounting guard.

Friday, 19 November
Shifted camp again. Dugouts swamped, prolonged
rain, marched full kit about two miles south to
Outerdam hut camp. Lying next 2nd Life Guards,
Lab. Batt. RE ASC. Huts very cold. Camp
fearfully muddy, lot of men sick with chilled feet,
boots good but socks wet every night.

Saturday, 20 November
In charge party dismantling old dugouts. Lance-
Corporal Tatlow stripped for 'DIS' *(?)*.

Sunday, 21 November
Corporal of Camp Guard. Armed guard during
night, picket during day. Weather very cold.

Tuesday, 30 November
On guard again. During night a Corporal of the
Lincolns, losing his way coming from trenches,
wandered to our Guard Room. Put him up, made
him tea, etc. Wet through, muddied and worn
out. Told such tales of suffering in trenches,
over knees in mud and water, bitter cold, bodies
and parts of bodies in the mud everywhere.
Shelled by our own artillery. Men's feet swelling
until boots burst.

Sunday, 5 December

Half day off. Our winter quarters very passable.
Huts (20 men) provided with stoves, the fire
making the long evenings very comfortable;
lounge and smoke, read, play cards and, if
inclined, convivial company at pub or canteen.
Served out with cardigan, mackintosh cape and
leather jerkin. Still on shellproof dugouts,
regularly in charge of party, concreting or
building with sandbags, rain most days, can take
shelter. Only drawback the confounded mud.

Wednesday, 8 December

On Guard, with Section 1. Corporal Madley a
prisoner.

Tuesday, 14 December

Recommended for promotion again. Witnessed air
duel today. British and German aeroplanes
manoeuvering for position, fighting with machine
guns. British worsted, plane down close to us,
machine crippled. Observer killed, pilot wounded.
Evident superiority of German machines.

Thursday, 16 December

On guard. Sec. 4. New Guard Room, roadside,
good one. My Section heavily shelled on job;
shrapnel. Sgt.Pennington wounded in head.
Sapper Pile wounded in hand. Paid 30 francs.

Saturday, 18 December

Promoted 2nd Corporal (In orders). Shilling a
day rank pay.

Sunday, 19 December

Engagement on Hooge Way, terrific bombardment
early morning. Germans use gas, cloud and shell.
Troops heavily shelled going up through Ypres.
Staffs. lose 120 men. Batteries shelled, four
officers killed together at battery near our job.
German attack fails.

Tuesday, 21 December

Rained all day, under shelter. Won 30 francs at
Brag.

Wednesday, 22 December
On Guard, double guard, 2 prisoners. In charge
of Corporal and Lance-Corporal.

Friday, 24 December
Finished job at 122 Battery.

Saturday, 25 December
Christmas Day: Work all day, 1¼-hour walk to
job on shellproof dugouts at 121 Battery with
Section 1. Poured with rain all way; fine all day.
Job off Kruisstraat, Ypres. People all gone from
village since here last. Every other house more
or less damaged. Dinner on return at 5.0, stew,
pudding, concert in evening. Officers and men. I
recited.

Monday, 27 December
Bad news from home. Kate in infirmary, diseased
hip. Applied to Sgt.Major for leave. Promised it
for first week in January. [*See previous entry of
15 July 1915.*]

Wednesday, 29 December
Section shelled on way to camp, shell burst few
yards from us, had to get away across fields.

Thursday, 30 December
Shelled on way home, same time and place. As
we cut across fields from road could see shells
bursting in old farm, close to battery.

Friday, 31 December
New Year's Eve. Our Section had orders pack
kits, paraded full marching order, to go to
Ramparts, Ypres. Our C.O., Major Wilson, called
me out. Was promoted Full Corporal December
31st, the third promotion in seven weeks.
Marched to Ypres, about six miles, relieved
Section 3. Mining dugouts in ramparts for
quartering reserve infantry. Am in charge of one
shift. A proper hell's corner for shellfire, but
galleries run 30 to 40 feet underground, so safe

from anything except Jack Johnson's *(a shell
bursting with black smoke, named after Negro
heavyweight boxing champion - 1908).* Interesting
bit of work, timbering, and comfortable billets.
Sleeping in galleries.

1915 – 1 year's soldiering – 1916

From sanatorium to the army. Dubious about
physical ability to stick it, training very trying
but condition gradually improved;   got through.

Soldiering pay one and tuppence per day. Passed
trade test as mason one and fourpence per day.

Four months at home (Anglesey) training. Been
now eight months in Flanders, working every
day, all classes of work, with exception of six
weeks down Line, in French cities of Le Havre
and Rouen. Touch of influenza. Run down, but
returned fit as ever again. Going through winter
campaign now. Hope to go through the war
now. Successive promotions Lance-, Second and
now Full Corporal, one and four a day, making
three shillings and tenpence a day in all.

Fairly satisfactory altogether.

Saturday, 15 January
Started away for nine days' special leave over young Katie. Drew £5 (140 francs), equipment and rifle. Walked to our new camp at Dikkebusch, then on to Poperinge, training at 5.0 a.m. dog-tired. Reached Boulogne 11.30. Over 1,000 of us marched up to Rest Camp 2 miles top of a hill, several hours. Caught boat 5 p.m.; all wore life-belts. Off boat onto train at Folkestone 7.0, London (Victoria) 8.30. Free refreshments, changed money, away by tube for Euston, bacon and eggs YMCA, train 12.10, Birmingham 3.0 a.m. Sunday morning. Sleeping waiting-room till 8.0. Then home after nine months. Wife and children.

Monday, 17 January
Erdington Infirmary. Saw Katie, looking well, under extension treatment for three or four months, then, if operation necessary, am to be communicated with.

Wednesday, 19 January
Went to Cheltenham, visited Dad, sister *(his elder sister Sue Knight)* and others. Seven days in England fairish time. Visited munition works. Soldiers everywhere, munition work everywhere, all else subordinate.

Saturday, 22 January
Saw Katie again. Caught train New Street 12.50. Euston 4.0 a.m. Walked across to Victoria, slept on platform, train 9.30, straight on boat at Folkestone, fine voyage. B*(?oulogne)* 12.30. Marched to Rest Camp. Eggs, bread and butter ninepence. Trained 8.0 p.m. Poperinge 1.0 a.m. Slept 'til 8.0, then long walk to camp, returning to Section, Ypres, evening.

Monday, 24 January
Back to Section, mining, Ypres ramparts. First night off, played Pontoon all night. Credit about £6.10.0.

Tuesday, 1 February

Went sick, ordered hospital. Waiting here in prison, Ypres F *(ield)* A *(mbulance)* dressing station, to be taken away. Feel really bad, cough increased, head bad, very short of wind.

Wednesday, 2 February

Advanced dressing station Poperinge. Brought here yesterday, slept overnight. Exam. again. Complaint changed from delmatitis *(?)* to bronchitis. Off again by ambulance car.

Thursday, 3 February

At Nunnery (Chateau Lovie) 16th Field Amb. Hell of a night. Internal stomach pains all afternoon. Earache all night, walking the ward. Exam. again. Head bad, cough still trouble. Marked for Gas Clearing Station. Most get sent up to Rest Camp for week. But I look bad enough; and need a rest.

Friday, 4 February

Move to 17th CCS Pop. Exam again. Bronchitis, marked Train. All equipment taken away again. Three months ago this happened before, or at least three months ago I returned from hospital. I was Sapper then, am (Act.) Full Corp. now. Away in the ambulance train, down the Line, mostly stretcher cases, wounded and sick. In my carriage there is typhoid, pleurisy and bronchitis. Orderlies and nurses move along the corridors in attendance.

Saturday, 5 February

Boulogne, 22 Gen. Hospital. Whirled here in a car from station late last night; bath, all clothes taken away, blue hospital suit given.

Monday, 7 February

Still in bed. Med. exam. today. Asked for history. Told of illness in S. Wales. Sputum test. Hospital, two converted hotels; Wimereux, suburb of Boulogne; the Metropole and Grand,

together about 400 beds. Medical staff all
Americans. Doctors and nurses very nice people;
no side. Concert by RAMC and staff last night.

Friday, 11 February
Before Colonel today. Marked out for Rest Camp.

Saturday, 12 February
Taken to 5 Conval. Camp by motor brake
(Boulogne).

Sunday, 13 February
Before Major RAMC. Light duty for few days.

Monday, 14 February
Orderly Sgt. for the Company. Pay: drew 10
francs. Well-regulated camp; food excellent.
Spring mattress beds in marquee.

Friday, 18 February
Company Inspection by C.O. Got 'Carry on' for
the present. Kennedy Rumford and Party
Concert. Lecture the previous evening.

Monday, 21 February
Still Acting Orderly Sergeant. A busy job but
rather interesting, detailing men for inspection,
fatigues, making out sick reports, etc. 66 men in
company, 1,000 men in camp.

Thursday, 24 February
Company Inspection by C.O. 'Carry on' again.

Sunday, 27 February
On pass to Boulogne from 2.0, couple mile stroll
along sea front and a drop of good whisky in the
evening. Won a few francs before turning in –
Brag.

Monday, 28 February
Wet – Canteen Corporal.

Tuesday, 29 February
Charge Fatigue Party No. 8 Gen. Hosp.

Wednesday, 1 March

C.O Inspection. Marked out 'Fit'. Base Details Camp, bell tents. Fatigues each day at docks, Boulogne. Parties leaving every day for the bases. First night, Corporal of the Guard.

Friday, 3 March

Ordered with party for Rouen. Marched with day's rations to station, 3.0 p.m. Trained in goods vans, cold and uncomfortable. Changed for 3 hours at Abbeville, feed in YMCA. Then long dreary night's ride, crawling pace, arriving tired out Rouen at 9.0 a.m.

Saturday, 4 March

Back again RE Base. This time as Corporal, included in Sergeants' Mess. Excellent food; 10 francs pay; cinema in evening.

Sunday, 5 March

Doctor's exam., marked 'Active'.

Monday, 6 March

Ammunition sheds Rouen; charge of gang.

Tuesday, 7 March

Jetty. New pier for unloading ammunition and guns. Charge gang of 30, carrying big timber.

Wednesday, 8 March

Went sick, toe trouble, chiropodist. Saw battalion of French conscripts, 1916 class, finest body of young men I have yet seen. Ruddy faces, strong-limbed, singing on the march. I notice numbers of new battalions of our chaps coming out, an undersized, narrow-chested lot, but heaps of British swank about them.

Friday, 10 March

Chiropodist tended my toenails.

Saturday, 11 March

Fatigue Party, Cavalry Base. Pay 20 francs.

Sunday, 12 March
Corporal Camp Guard. Lovely spring day; 77 passes issued. Couple of rowdy prisoners in evening.

Monday, 13 March
Evidence in three cases for Orderly Room; got two off.

Tuesday, 14 March
Charge of party, road-repairing, 5 Gen. Hospital.

Wednesday, 15 March
Pass to Rouen. Very fine city, extensive inland docks.

Thursday, 16 March
With 'fatigue party' to 19th Veterinary Hospital. Accommodation for 12,000.

Friday, 17 March
St. Patrick's Day. My birthday. With party of fifty to Indian Veterinary Hospital, acc. 14,000. On new stables and gravel pit.

Saturday, 18 March
With party of 100 to docks, timber carrying. Breakfast 6.15, Parade 6.45. Pay 10 francs on return.

Monday, 20 March
Docks, draining.

Tuesday, 21 March
With party 19th Veterinary Hospital.

Wednesday, 22 March
Corporal Camp Guard.

Thursday, 23 March
Day off, well-earned.

Friday, 24 March
Taking load old clothes, disinfect.

Saturday, 25 March
Jetty, timber shifting.

Sunday, 26 March
Jetty, 'til dinner time.

Monday, 27 March
Ammunition Depot, building sandbag buttresses between shell stores.

Tuesday, 28 March
Docks, unloading provisions with ASC dockers, heavy job, long day.

Wednesday, 29 March
With lorry, fetching timber, docks.

Thursday, 30 March
Jetty. In charge of cooks.

Saturday, 1 April
Docks. Supply Depot. Unloading ship, compressed hay.

Monday, 3 April
With lorry to docks for timber.

Tuesday, 4 April
Docks, unloading ship.

Thursday, 6 April
Docks again.

Friday, 7 April
Lorry; clinkers from destructor.

Monday, 10 April
Docks again.

Tuesday, 11 April
Glamorgans Camp; gardens.

Thursday, 13 April
Police duty; RE works.

Friday, 14 April

On escort duty, two prisoners 'Up the Line'. 2nd. Siege Coy.

Saturday, 15 April

Reached Hazebrouck 1.0 p.m. Reported to DA DRT *(Deputy Adjutant - Director of Railway Transport)*. Stayed at Reinforcements Camp. Handed prisoners over to Town Major. Spent evening in town; few drinks.

Sunday, 16 April

RTO *(Railway Transport Officer)* started us away for St. Pol 10.0 a.m., arrived 1.0 p.m. Reported RTO. Didn't know Coy. Sent us back to Hazebrouck. Caught leave train 10.0 p.m. Travelled all night.

Monday, 17 April

Changed St. Omer 4.30 a.m. Caught 8.30 and reported Hazebrouck 10.0 a.m. Sent up to Reinforcements Camp, drew rations, hung about office all afternoon; dismissed at 5.0 p.m. for the day.

Tuesday, 18 April

Reported DA DRT office 9.30 a.m. At 2.0 p.m. report again. Discovered moving order, started by 3.13 for Abbeville. Changed Calais 6 - 7. Strolled through town.

Wednesday, 19 April

Abbeville reached midnight. Reported RTO. Orders for morning. Roughed it in shed, equipment and men heaped up. Trained at 9.30 for unknown point. Prisoners' time expired but am to go on. Arrived little village station, railend, 4.00 p.m. Report RTO, sent on to Marieux six miles. No Coy. there, had left in lorry to Bethincourt. HQ 2nd Siege Coy. 7.00 p.m.

Thursday, 20 April

Warrant from Sgt.Major to return, with lorry, to

Doullens, fine old French town, 15 mile.
Reported RTO 10.30. Stroll through town and a
feed. Trained 2.10 for Rouen. Changed
Abbeville.

Friday, 21 April
Arrived camp 10.00 a.m. An interesting week's
tour of North France, covering about 500 miles.
A fine country. A stroll through Calais,
Hazebrouck and Abbeville. Ready to go to Coy.
any time now.

Saturday, 22 April
With party, RE yard.

Monday, 24 April
With party Rouen jetty, railway. Easter Monday:
with party, unloading ballast for new railway.
Evening: Concert Sgts.' Mess.

Tuesday, 25 April
With lorry over hills, brickyard. Beautiful view
of Rouen.

Wednesday, 26 April
Weight 10 st. 12 lb. Up the Line again to
Company after three months away.

Thursday, 27 April
Arrived Coy. Bethincourt between Arras and
Amiens. Somme district. Lovely country; low
hills, villages, orchards, a smiling countryside.
Six of our chaps wounded by shell today.

Friday, 28 April
Sent to Hébuterne, a deserted village, 400 yards
from Line, sinking and bricking shaft. Shift
work, dangerous place. Bullets and shells.

Sunday, 30 April
Bombardment last night. Continuous roar and
crash of shells and intermittent rattle of machine
guns. Billeted in old barn, expecting any minute

a shell to land into us. Fortunately we have a dressing station and a graveyard in this old village.

Monday, 1 May

Lovely weather, nature at her best, fruit trees in blossom, the love songs of birds. A pair of martins are building over my head, and every now and again a shell whizzes by or wrecks a cottage, or ploughs up a garden, and at intervals a German machine gun sweeps the village roads. And still the birds sing on.
Credit £14.

Sunday, 7 May

Rather like this place, building underground boilerhouse, billet in exposed position though. Sgt.Major and private killed here before we came. Bullets play round us occasionally. But locality is pretty and the weather grand.

Sunday, 14 May

Shift work, fixing pump 100 ft. down well.

Wednesday, 17 May

German bombardment last night; attack on our trenches. (T) Berks. 100 casualties, 30 killed; Glos. also suffered.

Thursday, 18 May

Rest of Sec. 2 came here; pipe-laying job; Pump St. to trenches. Playing Brag in the garden this evening. Machine-gun turned on us; threw ourselves on our faces; bullets hissed through bushes about us; not unusual this. Maxim most deadly, typical of modern machine warfare. No case of "familiarity breeding contempt" here.

Sunday, 21 May

Carrying pipes com*(munication)* trench. From one point got good view of trenches; their and our trenches mapped out below us; could observe our shells landing along their Line, and theirs in ours. Must have exposed myself to sniper; bullet hissed past my head.

Monday, 22 May

On early shift, 2.30 a.m. to 11.30 a.m. Laying and connecting pipes.

Wednesday, 24 May

Shrapnelled the village, had to take cover, sixty killed and wounded. Expected bombardment at night. Section scattered into cellars, proved a flat.

Thursday, 25 May

Village behind us, Sailly, shelled, over 100 casualties. The shell landed on group of children at play, killed 3, wounded 5. We were shelled at night, had to rush away. Took refuge in cellar all night.

Sunday, 28 May

Attack on our trenches. Shelled Héb *(uterne?)*; rush for cellar again.

Monday, 29 May

Section moved away. Full marching order, four miles along Line, to the Suchery. Another lively hole, another pipe-laying job in trenches.
Billeting Mailly, two mile back. Shelled going and coming to work. Shift 2.30 a.m - 1.30 p.m., very tiring.

Wednesday, 31 May

Mailly, where we billet, another pretty little country town, not yet shelled, bound to be later. Three miles from Line; but the Suchery where we pass is riddled with shells; been terrific fighting there between French and German, the latter held it. Our communication trenches run from it and the spot is shelled every day. Had couple of near things.

Wednesday, 7 June

Working nights now, laying pipes in the open

between trenches, away before the dawn. Under
fire from snipers and Maxims, our presence
disclosed by star–lights, bullets around us thick
last night. Kitchener drowned in *Hampshire*.
Naval battle, North Sea, May 31st. Mile of
trenches lost at Ypres.

Thursday & Friday, 8 & 9 June
Two awful wet nights, drenched to skin, plastered
with mud, rotten job to dry one's clothes.

Sunday, 11 June
Shelled us last night; Germans bombarded our
support trenches, shrapnelled our job too. Just
managed to get my party away, crawling along an
old trench, through barbed wire, wading through
water. Raining.

Monday, 12 June – Whit Monday
Left job early last night, bombardment expected.
Didn't come off.

Tuesday, 13 June
Another soaking last night.

Wednesday, 14 June
Digging trench near first line. Another wetting;
Army order for all blankets to be given in, sleep
in our clothing; .

Thursday, 15 June
First fine night; Maxim on us, just as we had
dug ourselves in. German star–lights wonderfully
efficient; a scythe of bullets swept the whole
trench.

Sunday, 18 June
On day shift, with party fixing pipes in new
trench and connecting tanks. Glorious weather;
all around beautiful country; in the distance the
occasional booming of guns; about this old
village the aspect of peace, except for the
batteries peeping here and there. On the eve of

our big offensive; tremendous preparations,
immense stores of big shells; everyone expectant.

Thursday, 22 June

With party last night, covering pipes. Our people
taking cylinders of gas into the trenches. Highly
dangerous job; wearing helmets. Been back eight
weeks now, feeling fine. Should like to stick it
now.

Saturday, 24 June

Ordered to move from village into open fields
nearby. Erected canvas bivouac. All civilians
cleared out of Mailly too. General scramble for
fruit, vegetables, poultry. Our bombardment
started. Scores of batteries around here
alternately keeping up line of fire on German
trenches.

Monday, 26 June

Sent with three chaps last night to follow the pipe
track for examination. Bombardment and
counter-bombardment on. Roar and crash.
Trenches in bad state, water and mud to knees.
Where pipes cross open ground between trenches,
apparently suicidal to venture. But orders must
be carried out. Light as day, what with star-
lights and the flashes of our guns behind us.
Hail of shrapnel and machine fire. Miles of
communication trenches to wade through between
Suchery and Hébuterne and back. Finished just
before dawn; then the gas started; donned
helmets and waded, stumbling, through the mud,
getting tangled with wires, fearful job to make
progress with helmet. One chap gassed; had to
help him along. Out on the road dodging
shrapnel. Cotterell left at dressing station:
Whittel of Section 4 killed near Suchery.
Germans shelling Mailly today. The picturesque
old village stands on hill facing us; watching
shells crushing buildings, raising clouds of dust.
The big building in centre on fire.

Tuesday, 27 June

Bombardment still going on, batts. of 12-in. and

9.2, also field batts. alternately keeping up the
fire. Sunday and Monday morning, lot of our
chaps killed with our own gas; Sunday a cylinder
was burst by shells. But Monday we tried gas
and the wind turned. That was the gas my party
encountered. Believe this morning our gas was a
success. Having a change in our diet, boiled
fowl, fresh vegetables, new potatoes, straw-
berries, lettuce. Loot, of course, but the
owners are gone, and the village is being
demolished.

Friday, 30 June

Advance put off for couple of days, 'to make
more sure', and the weather so bad. Germans
made bombing attack last two mornings,
indicating they possess very deep dugouts. How
anything could live under our bombardments of
the last week is marvellous. We are resting,
awaiting advance, so as to carry water pipes on;
practising fixing new pipes. Flange in place of
screw joints.

Saturday, 1 July

Terrific bombardment along this front early
morning; attack by 4th, 29th and *(illegible)* Divs.
10.00 a.m. streams of slightly wounded cases
returning. Rumours of British successes, German
1st, 2nd and 3rd line trenches taken. Villages on
right and left taken, village in front of us on fire.
Infantry advancing against hail of machine gun
fire. 4.0 p.m. Returning wounded telling tales of
Germans retaking lost trenches; we retiring from
our first line; defending our third line too. Job
to know what to believe. Anyway this 4th Div.
badly cut up; had to retire after taking trenches.
Maxims mowed them down in heaps. Official
British and French offensive, over 25 miles front,
the Somme. Hébuterne is the left flank. Progress
made Albert way, villages taken. But Germans
retook all positions on this 4-mile section, 3 Div.
cut up.
[*Editorial Note: 1st July. By nightfall on this
day, the British had suffered 60,000 casualties*

(19,000 dead) - the greatest loss by one side on any day of the war.]

Tuesday, 4 July

On sick list last four days, boil on shoulder, but went out last night with party to trenches to water tanks. Germans shelling Suchery and road outside comm. trenches. Return after midnight, just leaving comm. trench. Cutting through cemetery, raining, very dark. Shrapnel burst near us, I jumped into open grave just in time to dodge another; found it had an owner, a dead soldier lay there; crouching on the corpse, the darkness was lit up by another shell a couple of yards away; but I missed the shower of splinters. Poor chap, his open grave had probably saved my life. In hurrying away I stumbled against several other bodies awaiting interment. Matters at standstill here, but offensive continues down below; our advance checked here. Over fifty per cent of our men casualties. Awful state of our trenches; dead in heaps difficult to carry through comm. trenches. Germans shelling all the time our roads and comm. trenches.

Wednesday, 5 July

Half Section out last night; shoulder bad, couldn't go. Germans shelling approach to comm. trenches. Pemley *(?)* killed, W.C.Jones killed. Party failed to reach the job. Showers of shrapnel. Afternoon, fetched our two dead comrades back two miles across the shrapnel-swept plain from the Suchery. Buried them in little French cemetery near here amid the booming of the guns. Quite a tragic loss. Two of the nicest fellows in our Section.

Saturday, 8 July

Sgt. with party away bridging. Left in camp in charge of rest of Section. Burying our dead in heaps in old trenches owing to difficulty in getting them away. One heap of fifty just covered over in a disused trench, where they had been dumped; smelled awful.

Monday, 10 July

One of our wounded crawled in from 'tween trenches. Been out nine days. These civilised Christianised nations allowing their wounded to die in torture from exposure, actually firing on each other's collecting parties. Such is the value of 2,000 years of Christian teaching. Germans counter-attacking positions we have won down on the right. Trenches flooded after the rain, mud and water in places to the waist. This locality an inferno of shrapnel.

Wednesday, 12 July

Started another job. In charge of shift 4 - 12 a.m. Machine gun emplacements in old mill and new cellar dugouts in trenches. Dugout 15 ft. by 6 and 25 ft. down. Two stairway passages 3 ft. wide. All chalk ground. Timber sets at 45 degrees. Iron sheet revet*(ment)*.

Monday, 17 July

Back up here three months now, and a busy hot time at that. But am feeling more or less fed up. Men though working well not giving satisfaction. On this mining job experience of little value, must follow the book, work to the inch and push the job, too. Not feeling well either lately, bronchitis troublesome, boils on shoulder. Doctor gives me light duty but I go to the job. Another sergeant come to Section now straight from home depot!!!

Friday, 28 July

Right arm and hand swollen badly. Insect bite; attending doctor for left shoulder as well. As an NCO of course I can attend to duty. Still on cellar dugouts, 35 ft. down now. Chalk very decent stuff to work. Tim Murgatroyd Sec. 3 injured in camp, shell splinter. Draft of sixteen to Coy., two Sgts.

Sunday, 6 August

Mosquitoes still troubling. Arm the size of two. Also eye closed, boil, had to be lanced. Otherwise all right. Lovely weather, just the time for

lounging. Party No. 1 Section in trenches
Auchonvillers. Shell burst among them, five
casualties. Lieut. Danks and Sgt. Everton badly
wounded, Sapper Whitmore killed, another had
wrist smashed.

Tuesday, 8 August

Yesterday was Bank Holiday. How I spent it:
breakfast (bacon), lounge and a read; dinner
(stew); parade 11.30 - skeleton marching order;
equipment: ammunition, rifle, smoke helmet,
goggles, steel shrapnel helmet. Mile to job.
Shift from 12 - 8, mining block chalk. 25 ft.
below surface, stood set of timber. Return 8.0
p.m. tea, bread and jam, a game of Brag, then
turn in. Been month dugout; reserve line
trench.

Wednesday, 9 August

Another job. Front line trench, crater-facing.
Beaumont-Hamel. White City. Observation post
and cellar dugout. 1½ hours' walk, through
Auchonvillers. Afternoon shift, our guns shelling
the German trenches; can see them bursting
through sentries' periscope.

Friday, 11 August

Worked last night, over the top, roofing
O*(bservation)* P*(ost)*. Shelling back and fore all
night. Trench mortars make fearful noise and
crash. One killed, six wounded near us. One
bursting two traverses away knocked me down.
Wiring party near us, Maxim played on us,
stopped us working. Up and down for cover all
night. Damn nuisance trying to get bit of work
through.

Sunday, 13 August

Guards Brigade in trenches here, Scots,
Coldstreams and Grenadiers. Well supplied with
machine-guns. A wiring party by us had 31
casualties. Friday night we failed to work at all.
As soon as we mounted parapet and started, they

threw four whizz-bangs at us, dropped into handy
shell-hole. Then sentry called to us, "Look out,
trench mortar coming", we tumbled into trench as
with a roar the mortar burst on our left. From
then on all night a more or less continuous
supply, mortars, swish of Maxim bullets sweeping
along parapet, and the whizz-bangs in fours,
rapid. This Beaumont-Hamel we are facing, the
29th Div. attacked 1st July, but were cut up and
had to retire; the N. Lancs., who are working
with us, had 900 casualties in their battalion. We
exploded the biggest mine on this front.

Wednesday, 16 August

Just finished a two-nights' job. Making
O *(bservation)* Post in parapet on fire-step for
artillery o *(bservation)* on mine crater and
Beaumont-Hamel. Steel-plated roof and sides.
Bullets hissing around us; several explosive
bullets burst against sandbags close to us. Were
warned to have gas helmets handy as we were
going to use gas if wind favourable. Germans
kept up a fairly constant supply of trench mortars
and whizz-bangs. Terribly tiring, walking
through comm. trenches.

Thursday, 17 August

Worked afternoon, finish job. Last night
Shropshires, burying dead between lines: in
moving a British soldier caught in barbed wire
with bomb in his hand, the corpse's hand relaxed,
the bomb exploded, killing three of party.
IRONY OF FATE.

Thursday, 24 August

Couple of days off, waiting for job. Teeth
(artificial) broken. Reported to MO. Sent by
ambulance car to HQ Field Ambulance. Three of
us sent back, too many. Only 17 dental cases
allowed each week from 'Div'. Sapper Stavely
wounded. Party rejoined Section from Mencil.

Saturday, 26 August

Started deep dugout front line trench, off White

City. Am in charge afternoon shift. Mile to
trenches; then two miles of comm. trenches to
front line. Raining off and on several days.
Trenches in fearful state. Water and mud to the
knees. Terribly exhausting, wading through in
places a foot of mud.

Thursday, 31 August

Another try with teeth. Sent to 3rd F *(ield)*
A *(mbulance)* Bethincourt, then to 1st F.Am. Buss,
wrong day; come again.

Saturday, 2 September

A hot time in trenches yesterday, Germans
shelling our front line all afternoon. Roumania
declares war on Central Powers.

[*Editorial Note: The declaration of war was on
27 August, so war news took a few days to reach
the troops.*]

Sunday, 3 September

Relieved by Sec. 5. We return to Headquarters,
Bertrancourt. Continuous bombardment all last
night and today; we are trying to take Thiepval.
(Failed to take Thiepval – heavy casualties.)
Entered 1st Field Amb. (S. Midland) Buss for
dental treatment. Dental Surgeon, Lieut. Bowater
(son Lord Mayor of Birmingham). Number of
our 'Special Gas Coy.' coming in gassed. Three
parts of 8th Worcesters (T) gassed by new
German gas shell; supposed to affect lungs.

Tuesday, 5 September

Returned to Section, having week's rest; hour's
drill morning. Applied to C.O., obtained special
pay for Section. Having a good time.

Sunday, 10 September

Left HQ for Englebelmer. Section camped side of
hill, under canvas. Job, H. *(?)* trench mortar
gun emplacement. Comm. trench facing Thiepval
Wood. Shift work continuous. 13th Glosters

with us. A week ago we attacked here for
Thiepval, but failed (facing valley of the Ancre).

Friday, 15 September

Wounded private crawled in today from between
trenches, 'No Man's Land'; out since attack 12
days ago!! Night off; attack coming off. A
merry evening at anti-aircraft canteen. Am in
charge of night shift, excavating gun emplacement in the open. Twenty infantry under me too.
Scores of shell craters all about us, disposing of
muck in them. Biggish job, emplacement 20 ft.
by 18 ft., 20ft. deep. 8 ft. square in bottom.

Sunday, 17 September

Fine spectacle last night. Our job commands good
view of German and British trenches, running
parallel up hillside by Thiepval Wood. At regular
intervals star-lights go up, light up the blackness,
then die away, but they only give away moving
figures. Englebelmer *(In margin)*. A bombing
attack was on and a regular exchange of shrapnel
took place. The sharp vicious crash of bursting
shrapnel echoing in the valley; and the lesser
crash, crash of the bombs. A bursting shell at
night is a spectacle, a blinding flash denoting its
locality; by day it is a cloud of dirt and smoke.
This is a splendid panorama from here but awful
when one considers that human flesh is the target.
The awful grandeur of the spectacle, the terrible
meaning of it all.

Wednesday, 20 September

Started day shift, six hours on job, an hour
walking each way. Rain off and on every day;
very cold too. Fine weather finished now. Cold
and wet, mud and water everywhere. If lucky
enough not to get wet through with rain, wet feet
every day. Every job in the trenches now;
nearly all mining work. Don't expect to last long
under these conditions but will stick it as long as
possible.

Monday, 25 September
Twelve months ago went down line sick. Weather has suddenly recovered, sunshine every day, roads and trenches dried up.

Tuesday, 26 September
Went to the job; no infantry turned up; no working parties were supposed to be in trenches, as attack was coming off; we shouldn't have been out. Worked till 1.00 when suddenly terrific bombardment started, heavies, field-guns, mortars, etc.; and a great cloud of poison gas went up just in front of us and moved over towards the German lines. The din was deafening; one could see our shells bursting in a line along the G*(erman)* trenches; the Germans answering, shells were dropping in our "supports" just behind us, Maxims were rattling. I started back with my party. A shell burst just in front, blocking the trench; we climbed over it and on, then one burst just behind us. But we got away safely after all. Thiepval taken, also Combles. This t*(rench)* m*(ortar)* emplacement needed for attack on Beaumont-Hamel.

Wednesday, 4 October
Courcelles, Section moved to Headquarters. Making railway siding, Colincamps. Billeting in old barn.

Friday, 6 October
Pay - Credit last June £17.
[*In margin:* October 9th Son born. *This was George, who died only three months later. See diary entry of 23 January 1917.*]

Friday, 13 October
Heavy bombardment of the plain to the right front of us; shells bursting all about battery by Suchery. Transports dashing for cover. This is biggish job, 200 men on it, a third of a mile of siding, heavy stone foundation, foot of ground to excavate. Train-loads of metal to discharge daily. Infantry (Black Watch and Worcesters) assisting.

Sunday, 15 October
Job shelled off and on all day; expect we shall
touch out shortly.

Monday, 16 October
Courcelles. Sunshine all day, first-class for
aeroplane observation; watched a fine air duel.
German machine distinctly superior. Fight to the
death. Fritz brought ours down. One killed, the
other passed us, head bandaged. G *(erman)* planes
up great height, but seemed to avoid our shrapnel
easily.

Thursday, 19 October
Rain. Parade 10.30, raining all day, job shelled.

Wednesday, 25 October
Broke art *(ificial)* teeth. Saw doctor. 'Get them
repaired after the War.' The average army doctor
regards the average sick man as a malingerer! the
many suffering for the few. The rainy season has
set in; drizzle, drizzle, cold, fearful mud
everywhere.

Thursday, 26 October
Away day, Hébuterne, with 10 sappers and 25
infantry, building sandbag wall against pumping
station. Shrapnel flying about us. This village
three parts demolished. Full of troops back in
the spring. Billy Veal (Sec. 1) killed at Suchery.
Big air fight over Hébuterne. Several planes
brought down, 3 German and 2 British (British
Off. R.). *(?)*

Saturday, 28 October
New job. In charge of detachment, 16 men,
building stables at Couin - away behind the line in
village on a hill; civilians here. No shellfire;
only transports everywhere, feeding the line,
munitions, food, material, drawing rations, HQ
13th A Corps. Billeting at old farm, barn.

Wednesday, 1 November
Very comfortable here (Couin), comfortable billet,

good cook appointed. Sole charge – rations, discipline, etc., all carpentering jobs. Good officer. Roofed a stable 900 sheets c *(orrugated)* iron.

Saturday, 11 November
Finished another stable, wire and felt.

Monday, 13 November
Terrific bombardment. Big attack today, on this front. Attempt to force the Gommecourt Beaumont-Hamel Section, which held us July 1st. Took Beaumont-Hamel and Beaucourt, failed at Serre.

Saturday, 18 November
Furious fighting all the week, Germans fiercely counter-attacking. Mud, then frost, terribly cold, snow today.

Monday, 20 November
Fixing billets and stable in Goineux *(?)*.

Wednesday, 22 November
On Bow portable huts, St. Leger Road. Attached to 13th Corps Headquarters, but Corps shifting next week, so our job coming to a close. Fixing two stables for batteries; laundry, baths, drying sheds, Couin. We have bath every Friday, change of clothes at laundry, half day every Sunday. First class rations from Corps HQ. Good cook; pudding every other day, biscuits for flour in suet pudding.

Wednesday, 29 November
Finished up. Marched back to the Coy. 3 miles, been away month. Coy. moved back to former camp.

Thursday, 30 November
Bertincourt. Coy. on hut building and road repairs. In camp first day. Fixing field-oven for cooks.

Saturday, 2 December
Sawmill Ber. *(?)* Shifting engine.

Sunday, 3 December
In camp, on drying shed.

Monday, 4 December
Appointed Company Orderly Corporal. My first
staff job. Letter from Dad saying brother
George, Lieut. Canadian Infantry, wounded on 18
November, shell wound mouth and abdomen. [*Died
London 20.12.16, aged 33 – see diary entry of 5
January 1917 and Appendix IV.*]

Wednesday, 6 December
Germans take Bucharest, capture oilfields and
grain districts. British Cabinet resigns. Lloyd
George to form new Cabinet.

Monday, 18 December
On Orderly Corporal a fortnight now; a busy job
too: blow the 1/4 dress at 7.15. Round to
Officers' Mess, fetch letters, blow the 5 minutes.
Parade HQ Section; call roll, etc., names of sick,
make out s*(ick)* reports, hang around Orderly
Room, detailing men and transport for jobs 'til
dinner–time. Couple of hours off in afternoon
(perhaps), called every now and again to find men
for loading or unloading. After tea, warn Guard;
attend Orderly Room about 5 to 7, transmit
orders for new jobs, etc. At 7 collect letters and
take Officers' Mess, at 9 call the roll and read
orders. Then report to Coy. Sgt.Major. Go
round and report C.O. Then do as I like.

Monday, 25 December – Christmas Day
Day's holiday. But I was busy enough all day.
Had a gay time Christmas Eve, champagne, rum,
etc., drinking everyone's health; self and Orderly
Sergeant tumbling over each other calling the roll.
Took all Christmas Day to recover. Running
about all day with orders. Drank healths with
officers in Mess to finish a busy day.

Tuesday, 26 December – Boxing Day

Another busy day, Coy. moving away a few miles back again. Sgt.Major and C.O. away on leave, meaning a lot of extra work. Changing with the 135 Coy. from Doullens, army, troops, work. Hell of a nuisance, shifting camp.

Friday, 29 December

Moved Doullens. Coy. HQ in the town; men mostly away on detachments in neighbouring villages; hut building. Still Orderly Corporal (a month now). About the town every day on duty. Fine old French provincial town. HQ 5th Army Corps; we are attached.

Monday, New Year's Day, 1917

Complete two years' soldiering. One year a Full Corporal. Had a most strenuous year in France, six months working in the trenches, Somme District, during the offensive. Mining and water supply work, mostly in sole charge of party. Feel as fit as ever I did and ready for the coming spring offensive again.
Looking forward to a leave shortly.

Friday, 5 January

Letter from Dad. Brother George died from
wounds Wednesday, December 20, London. Sick
with lower a *(rtificial)* teeth again. Dentist breaks
them, takes impression and I am to have another
lot. *(In margin:* Received teeth January 19th.)

Friday, 12 January

Back into 13th A Corps, who have moved here in
place of 5th Corps.

Wednesday, 17 January

New troops pouring out here in readiness for
spring offensive. Country white with snow;
snowing all day. Couldn't have a better job this
season, handy little hut, good stove, hours during
day for reading, etc.

Tuesday, 23 January

Anniversary of enlistment; not the remotest idea
two years ago that I would be here now. The
END apparently as far off as ever. This summer
should see the BREAK. Want to go through to
the end, feel fit enough. Anniversary of listing
two years ago. DEATH OF MY BOY GEORGE.
The lad is better off; he is free from wage
slavery and the insults of class rule.

Saturday, 10 February

Here six weeks now, Doullens. For a month
everything frozen up, terribly cold; but fine, sun
by day, clear starry sky by night. The winter
slipping away very comfortably, always a good
fire and good food. Still Company Orderly
Corporal. Asked to go away on a job, no notice
taken; bronchitis rather troublesome, want to
avoid falling sick. In hospital this time last year
with it. Want to be out here for the big spring
offensive for which I see such tremendous
preparations being made.

Sunday, 11 February

Handed over Orderly Corporal.

Monday, 12 February

New job again. Ration and Post Corporal. Really Deputy Quartermaster. With transport drawing rations from Supply HQ, mornings. Fetching mail, afternoons, issuing stores between. Most interesting work.

Monday, 19 February

Letter today saying daughter Katie cannot live long; saddest blow of my life this. Application for special leave.

Monday, 26 February

Warned 10 p.m. to go on leave; hasty pack-up. Paid £5, station 1.45 a.m., train late, got away 4.0 a.m., reached Boulogne 12 noon. Fearful journey, tried to sleep, feet frozen, windows broken, hungry, no chance of refreshment. Taken, twenty of us specials, to rest house. Wash, shave, a feed, away to boat at 4 p.m.

Tuesday, 27 February

Crossed to Folkestone, 4 - 6. Trained to Victoria, London 8.30. Rotten tired. Bed at YMCA, Euston. Supper and breakfast.

Wednesday, 28 February

Birmingham at 12 noon. Visited infirmary afternoon. Katie better again. [*Note: This daughter in fact survived for another 67 years.*]

Saturday, 3 March

Carbuncle in neck very painful. MO, Military Hospital, Dudley Road, lanced it. Attend every morning for dressing. Most infernal nuisance, neck in bandages.

Tuesday, 6 March

Visited Cheltenham, Dad and sister.

Thursday, 8 March

Infirmary afternoon, hospital morning. Train evening at 7 p.m., latest for London. Euston 11.

Put up S*(alvation)* A*(rmy)* Soldiers' Hotel.

Friday, 9 March
Trained for Folkestone at 8, where we were
interned at rest camp, fearfully cold, snowing.
Away at 3 p.m. Fine passage, slept all the way.
Marched to rest house Boulogne at 5 p.m.
Interned 'til next day (prisoners of war).

Saturday, 10 March
Away up the Line 10.30 a.m.. Detrained Etaples.
Waited two hours. Marched during afternoon up
the hill to Etaples rest camp overnight. Under
canvas. Cinema during evening.

Sunday, 11 March
Trained again at 8. In trucks. Fourteen hours'
monotonous travel. 10 p.m. Railhead, Askew
(? Ascq), night rest camp.

Monday, 12 March
Job to get Coy. located, RTO didn't know, HQ
5th Corps Chief Engineer informed me we had
gone up the Somme. Tramped about 14 miles
through mud, full kit. Passed Albert and the old
German First Line, through ruined Ovillers, on to
Coy. at Pozieres. Canvas camp in the mud;
everywhere ground hit up in heaps, stumps in
place of trees, ruined trenches, a foot showing
out of the earth here, BODIES EVERYWHERE
JUST UNDER THE SOIL. Lost my staff job, out
with Section. Eight casualties yesterday, Corporal
killed, two Sergeants wounded, five Sappers
wounded.

Tuesday, 13 March
Day off, diarrhoea. *(In margin:* Pozieres*)*.

Wednesday, 14 March
Out with Section again, working roadmaking at
Courcelette. 3/4 hour walk, roads very bad.
Rained all day; using material from wreckage.
Ground around village one vast battlefield. Bodies

lying unburied everywhere. Legs, arms, feet in every heap of ruins. Canadians and Germans changed possession many times; house-to-house fighting.

Saturday, 17 March
Birthday, lovely day. We take Bapaume and Achiet-le-Petit. Can see smoke from the captured town from where we work.

Sunday, 18 March
Half holiday. Promoted SERGEANT, thus at last attaining the position I had aspired to since coming out. Each step of promotion won actually IN THE FIELD. Present pay: Soldier Pay one and tuppence, Trade Pay one and fourpence, Rank Pay two and a penny, Total four shillings and sevenpence.

Wednesday, 21 March
Near Petit Miraumont. Road torn up; great gaping shell-holes; timbering them over, material from old dugouts. British and German dead strewn about partly buried. Wrecked field-gun, seven mounds; as they fell! German and Canadian lying, each bayonet through the other. Wonderful German dugouts 30 ft. deep. Thousands of rifles, hand grenades, bombs lying about used and unused, dangerous to touch. My party exploded a bomb by touch of shovel. Salvage companies hard at it, collecting material. Lamentable part of it is that most of the material is unused – shells, bombs, equipment. What strikes one is the colossal waste of war.

Thursday, 22 March
Snow, blizzards during the day. Day off, with GS *(General Service)* wagon to Albert to purchase goods for canteen and Sgts.' mess. Albert old French town badly damaged by shellfire, mostly shrapnel; bronze statue of Virgin with Child hanging from spire. [*Dislodged by bombardment in January 1915.*]

Saturday, 24 March
> In front of Piz *(? Pas - East of Doullens),* making
> road. Terrible fighting here last month.
> Timbering over shell–holes, graves all around.

Tuesday, 27 March
> Struck camp for away up line. Following advance,
> marched about eight miles. Pitched camp under
> Bapaume Ridge, near villages of Thilloy *(?*
> *Tilloloy)* and Ligny. Range of hills, guns going
> day and night, fearful cold, mud, rain and
> blizzards.

Friday, 30 March
> Working in Bapaume. The old French town (rail
> junction), though evacuated by the Germans, is
> absolutely wrecked, not a building tenantable, the
> most thoroughly systematic destruction. Cross-
> roads mined, trees felled, rails lifted, everything
> of military value removed. Town Hall blown up
> the other day, Ger*(man)* agency, lot of British
> casualties. We are attached to ANZAC *(Australian*
> *and New Zealand Army Corps).* Our present
> work is a light railway.

Sunday, 1 April
> In charge party laying 'Decaville' light railway,
> shift 12 - 8, for conveying ammunition to
> batteries. Line running through Bapaume town;
> advance parties levelling, demolishing walls.
> Watched German 'plane drop bomb on our
> ob*(servation)* balloon. Was Ord.Sgt. this day, but
> taken off for this job.

Monday, 2 April
> Heavy snowstorm, stopped work.

Tuesday, 3 April
> Finished the line, worked 10 - 9. Watched quite
> close Ger*(man)* Taube *(Taube = Dove, so called*
> *from shape of the wings; 2-seater monoplane)*
> swoop down, fire on observation balloon, then
> wheel along and repeat the operation on another;

then away. Flying low and 'planing in and out,
shrapnel bursting all around him, he just got
away. The most astounding audacity I have seen
in two years out here, we stood spellbound;
everybody expressing admiration for the daring
ability.

Wednesday, 4 April
German airman who busted observation balloon
shot down today.

Thursday, 5 April
Ord.Sgt. Good day in camp.

Friday, 6 April – Good Friday
Packing light railway. Morning shift 4.30 – 1.30.

Saturday, 7 April
Snow and rain all day, in camp.

Sunday, 8 April
Early morning bombardment beyond Bapaume.
With daybreak, beyond ridge in front of us, a line
of flashes and a roar of guns. Then later gangs
of prisoners passing us

Monday, 9 April – Easter Monday
Fearfully cold, icy sleet cutting across the plains.

Tuesday, 10 April
. Fresh job, Grevillers village. Australian No. 5
CCS *(Casualty Clearing Station)*, fixing latrines,
stores, platforms. Snowing all day. Hospital
train loading up with Anzacs.

Wednesday, 11 April
Fixing stores in marquees, watching operations,
dressings, etc. Wounded terribly cut about.
Impressed with modern surgical science.

Thursday, 12 April
Camp Ord *(erly)* Sgt. Rain and snow again.

Germans retook villages from Australians. Aus.
75% cas. *(? casualties).* These Anzacs a fine body
of men; fine physique generally; strong faces;
breezy manner. The free open-air life is well
reflected and the rebel stock is easily noticeable.
Good comradeship, no petty individual bickering.

Friday, 13 April
Another job, at Fresnicourt, road-making, pipe-
track, water tanks, 5-mile walk. Keystone drill-
sinking nearby. Fixing up water supply plant, an
important factor in an "advance".

Sunday, 15 April
German counter-attack, took about sixty field
guns of the Anzacs and 1,000 men but we retook
them same day.

Wednesday, 18 April
Fearful weather; two days' rain, icy cold, mud,
height of misery, working all day in it; marching
in rain-soaked overcoat and equipment.

Thursday, 19 April
Ord.Sgt. for the day. A rest after the long drag
to the job. Out here two years next month; had
doubts about sticking two months. Earned promotions Lance-, Second and Full Corporal, then
Sergeant; had a month this rank. This was
worth working for too. The responsibilities of
the rank are not the least of the advantages. The
handling of men and the running of jobs, without
the fatigue of hard manual labour, the moving at
will from one part of the job to another, these
things render the post worth the having without
the extra money. But the satisfaction of climbing
step by step upwards to the point desired is the
greatest satisfaction of all. I may lose it any day
quite easily. But that will be a small matter,
having achieved one's object.

Sunday, 22 April
Finished water job at Fresnicourt.

Monday, 23 April

Orderly Sergeant. Lovely spring day. Did my washing and dried it. 'Bon'.

Tuesday, 24 April

Covering shell holes on Thilloy-Bapaume road *(? Tilloloy)*.

Wednesday, 25 April

Struck camp for Beugny. Sec. 2 & 3 forming right half coy., the others forming left half at Hermies. On Bapaume-Cambrai road about six miles. Marched full equipment, fine day.

Sunday, 29 April

On morning shift 4 - 12.30. Keystone well, pipe-laying, troughs, etc.; lovely weather, charge of two Sections.

Wednesday, 2 May

Job shelled today, one shell caught railhead; another landed amongst horses, lifted one 50 ft., others dropped by water tanks, ammo. *(= ammunition)* dump. We had to clear away for an hour.

Friday, 4 May

Day shift again, 7.30 - 4.30, sweltering hot day; played football this evening; just had bath, shell-hole.

Saturday, 5 May

Shelling job off and on all day. One hit railway, ripped up 6 pair rails. One just missed by yards big water tanks, our chaps working on them at time. German 'plane over camps after dark; dropped bombs into Bapaume, then returning flying low (could just see him), played a machine-gun on our camp. We hear he also attacked troops on the highway.

Monday, 7 May

With party fixing and covering elephant shelter

(semi-circular-sectioned shelter made of curved sheets of corrugated iron) over pump plant, 6.30 - 4.00. Four-foot sandbags.

Saturday, 12 May
Very hot weather. Feel uncomfortable, got idea that I have put my foot into it somehow; relationship with officers strained. Don't seem to give the same satisfaction. Can see the clouds burst any day. Am prepared any time now. New scenes and conditions wouldn't be amiss.

Monday, 21 May
Rained all day; wet through.

Tuesday, 22 May
Shelled on way to camp. One shell landed six yards from Section. Then shelled out of camp, afternoon.

Saturday, 26 May
Inoculated, 48 hours' rest. Sec. 2 Sgt. away, in charge dump. Am in charge Sec. 2 now.

Monday, 28 May
Making timbered road for standpipes.

Friday, 1 June
Thilloy - again. Back to HQ, left ANZAC, attached 4th Corps.

Saturday, 2 June
Another job, Bapaume-Arras road, amm *(unition)* dump. Erecting sandbag buttresses 'tween stacks, each taking 2,500 bags, 40 infantry.

Sunday, 3 June
Half-day, football match with Anglesey Rail. Coy., drew 2 - 2. Shelled as our motor lorry sailed through Fresnicourt. One just missed car.

Sunday, 10 June
Three days off with eye. Attending ANZAC

doctor at Bapaume. Glorious weather, feeling
quite fit. No sign of war finishing before winter.
Each attempt to smash through seems abortive:
Somme, Vimy Ridge, Arras, Bullecourt and now
Ypres. A smash of a strong position at
tremendous cost, then a deadlock. Tilloy.

Monday, 11 June

With party erecting Nissen huts at 4th Corps HQ
– Grevillers. Grevillers a beautiful village once,
now a complete wreck, every house shattered,
trees broken, systematically destroyed by the
Germans. Every house surrounded by garden and
trees – an ideal garden city. Germans must have
had a fine time here. Wine and spirit bottles
lying about. Deep dugouts here and there, old
gun positions, powerfully built.

Wednesday, 20 June

New job, Bapaume; small party RE's, 80
Australian inf *(antry)*, making RE dump, huts,
offices, sheds, on site of old German amm *(unition)*
stores. Roof of concrete 18 inches, reinforced
with steel rails and wire, covered steel plates. On
retirement Germans dropped the roof, now
hundreds of tons to break up and shift; takes
slab of gun cotton for every yard. Building big
wall with concrete blocks.

Sunday, 24 June

Religious service on – just two years since we had
one. We are still praying and still fighting, yet
neither seems to have any effect. Military
situation very much the same, the end apparently
as far off as ever. Yet what thousands of
millions wasted, what rivers of blood! The
Revolution in Russia the only bright spot. [*Note:
The Tsar had abdicated in March 1917.*]

Sunday, 1 July

Sgts.' Mess (Tilloy). After service the chaplain
(Capt.) came in, had a lot to say to everyone
about the glorious achievements of the British,

etc., etc. A regular fighting parson. Couldn't resist the temptation; we had hammer and tongs argument for an hour and a half, plenty of heat, too; provided sport for the others. Finished up the evening with bottle of stout.

Sunday, 8 July

Here it is again, another example of why we don't beat the Germans. My job, RE Park Bapaume, practically finished. Now all erections to be pulled down, stores, huts, etc., after six weeks' labour; light 'Decaville' track to be laid about, a new plan drawn. Yet tramway people say a slight deflection of lines would miss the buildings. But Chief Engineer says, 'All must come down.'

Tuesday, 10 July

Shelled today, high velocity shells dropping in front of us and to the right, man injured, foot. Evidently after railway which runs two sides of us; used to shell here heavily.

Wednesday, 11 July

Shelled job today. We had narrow escape, 2 killed, 3 injured within couple of yards of us; one man with head blown away. Inf *(antry)* Sgt. killed. Applied first aid to injured men.

Thursday, 12 July

Super German dugout on my job, evidently staff officers' quarters, 100 ft. deep, 3 entrances, 7 stairways, 3 landings, 5 bedrooms off the bottom one, rooms lined, polished wainscotting, lit with electricity; dining hall luxurious.

Saturday, 14 July

Sgt.Major Mignett went hospital. Mess supper and smoker. Bottled beer, port wine, champagne. Quite a good evening.

Tuesday, 17 July

Grevillers, Corps HQ. Charge party taking down Greenly huts, worked on till 8.30.

Wednesday & Thursday, 18 & 19 July
The same and loading away, 4th Corps moving to Etricourt *(?)*.

Saturday, 21 July
No. 7 RE Park to be pulled down again; after twice building it and system of light railways laid through it.

Tuesday, 24 July
La Boiselle (Detach.). Away. Evening, stroll around battlefields of July 1 - 16, Contalmaison, Fricourt, Mametz, etc. Little white crosses dotted everywhere over the slopes fronting old German front line. Mounds with 20 or 30 names, DCLI, TCL, SWB.

Wednesday, 25 July
With party Sappers RE & Herts. Inf., with 100 Indian hill tribesmen (Himalayan). Pulling down Nissen hut camps and loading away to be sent up line; huts housed troops last winter; moved up for troops this next.

Thursday, 2 August
Weather wet and cold; wet through today; these hillmen require lot of looking after, can do lot of work; carrying loads long distances.

Monday, 6 August - Bank Holiday
Rolled out of bed (wire-covered wood frame) at 6; batman brought in our bacon and tea. Grand clear morning. Parade at 7. Met our party of Indians, then away along the road over Contalmaison Hill to hill overlooking Fricourt. Busy all day keeping 10 motor lorries going, loading huts for railway siding. Shouting at Indians like a slave driver. Return to camp 3.30. Dinner, the usual stew, then tea, bread, butter, jam, smoke and the book. Came on wet evening so lit stove, then lounge and read till turn in. Other evenings we relieve things with shooting or ratting with the old dog.

Saturday, 11 August

Dropping huts at Fricourt. 150 Germans (war prisoners) and 50 Indians. Germans good steady workers, at least a score speak English. Armed guard.

Saturday, 18 August

On 200 huts at Becourt *(?)*, 100 Indians, dropping, carrying, loading on dump for transit up line. Plenty of fruit here, plums, apples, blackberries.

Wednesday, 22 August

On Crucifix Camp, Fricourt, charge of labour company (200) fresh from England. Mostly conscripts (Jews), a few 'unfits', an ALIEN company in fact.

Sunday, 26 August

Day off; had a ramble to Thiepval, and Beaumont-Hamel, the two strongest German fortresses on this front, both honeycombed with tunnels and forts, the dominating ridges dotted with concreted machine-gun emplacements. But the slopes leading to these places are dotted with thousands of British graves.

Wednesday, 29 August

Day trip to Amiens; old historic capital of Picardy. Grand cathedral, wide thoroughfares and avenues.

Saturday, 1 September

Fresh camp Mametz Wood. Scramble with Australian deserters armed with rifles. Nabbed one but he got away with the rest. We were unarmed; arrested camp warden, 'harbouring'. They had been living in style, robbing wardens in these deserted camps, breaking into stores, etc.

Sunday, 2 September

Deserters rounded up and caught. I with party helped beat through the wood. This Mametz

Wood full of German dugouts. Welsh Div. badly cut up taking this.

Thursday, 6 August

Dropping camps Bagentin *(?)* High Wood, close to where burial party lately buried 800 bodies. All these positions terribly hard to take, trees all ripped to stumps. Visited Delville Wood, Longueval. Bodies here yet unburied – in heaps.

Saturday, 8 September

Coy. gathered at HQ for 1000th day celebration. What a 'do'! Free drinks for all, beer, champagne, whisky, whist drive, concert, speeches; asked to be correspondent for *Sapper.*

Sunday, 9 September

Evening in Albert cafés, British, French, Yankees.

Monday, 10 September

Sent with party to HQ. With hutbuilding party, French huts, a CCS, Grevillers. Had 7 weeks in Albert dist. on huts, an interesting time, had in turn Indians, Germans and conscript alien Jews.

Wednesday, 12 September

Whist drive and concert, at Bagentin, 12-mile lorry trip. Camp Sergeant now, damn monotonous job.

Saturday, 15 September

. Concert and supper.

Friday, 21 September

Football started, organizing team. Played 4th Corps Cyclists, won 4 – 1.

Thursday, 27 September

Us v 29th CCS: won 1 – 0. News that the Depot Beaumaris is cleared, including drill instructors, and transferred to infantry, York & Lancs. Out here too Departmental Corps are being combed out, REs, motor transport, etc.

Am quite indifferent about the matter; a change
if only into a fighting unit has its attractions.
Credit June £19.6.0.

Sunday, 30 September
Played ROD, won 2 - 0.

Tuesday, 2 October
Waiting dental treatment, repairs. Beaulencourt;
c/o London Field Ambulance. Marched party 25
from 'Decaville' Detraining Centre, Bapaume, about
3 miles, all dental cases. Lovely day, clear sky,
had month fine weather. Patients all lying outside
in the sun. Gentle west wind blowing. Am in
charge of party building our winter camp; looks
as if we are staying here.

Monday, 8 October
Detachment - Villers-au-Flos. Sent with party to
reinforce party there. Sgt.Edwards and I with 53
REs and 200 labourers, Cyclists Corps & Lab *(our)*
Coy., building huts for 4th Army Corps HQ
around an old ruined château. These staff
quarters the last word for comfort. Greenly,
Nissen and *(?)* and Armstrong huts, but the
extras - matchboard lining, canvas, rubber felt,
brick fireplaces instead of stoves! Nothing too
good or too expensive for them. Compared to
the billeting of troops this is a scandal. Such an
abundance of material that is wellnigh impossible
to get for other jobs requiring it. We billet in
the old château, surrounded by giant oak, chestnut
and elm trees. Another garden village but
wrecked like the other evacuated places.

Sunday, 14 October
Team played 4 Corps Cyclists, 1 - 1,

Monday, 15 October
Rigged a bed upstairs in the old ruined château;
roof and walls broken, windows blown out; the
wind howls through the old ruins and the rain
beats in but I breathe the keen air and pity the

others in the vitiated atmosphere of the over-crowded room below. In charge party of joiners, navvies and cyclists, excavating and building latrines. Navvies – aged between 40 and 60, damn good men. Cyclists – young chaps, swanky and lazy.

Saturday, 20 October
Our chaps working late each evening. Corps moving in tomorrow. Staff Officers' Mess luxury itself. Weatherboarded hut, lined damp-proof paper, then matchboarded, then oak-panelled, with a double floor. And these old navvies, sleeping in tents, with just a ground sheet on the damp earth.

Saturday, 27 October
Report to Town Major Albert. Summary of evidence re 'harbouring deserters' case. 32-mile return. Lifts by motor lorries.

Sunday, 28 October
Team v 3rd *(?)* Railway Coy., 5 – 2.

Saturday, 3 November
Finished here. Charge of making 40 latrines for HQ. Navvies very satisfactory workers.

Sunday, 4 November
Full marching order, report Hun dump Leir *(?)* Viner, pick up timbers for a job, and away. Attached to 336 Road Construction Coy., RE Bertincourt. Job at Velu Wood, bridge giving way, main road. Party dozen Gen. Service men. Timber from the wood, heavy box drain. Cog off it up to bridge, heavy work; men not much use, ALL 'UNFITS', do the work myself. *(In margin:* Commended by C.O.*)*.

Monday, 5 November
Germans shelling the wood just above us.

Friday, 9 November
Finished bridge in pouring rain..

Saturday, 10 November
Returned HQ.

Sunday, 11 November
Summoned Albert, court martial, chief witness,
'harbouring deserters' case. Very unpleasant job;
didn't like it at all.

Monday, 12 November
Charge party building prisoner-of-war camp,
Bapaume.

Wednesday, 14 November
Heavy bridging course, Hun dump, Coy. on
bridging during this push.

Thursday, 15 November
Dump morning, marching orders for Beaumetz.
Travel by light railway, fearful cold, took from
6.00 to 9.00. Charge of bridge 10h *(?)* till the
'DO'.

Saturday, 17 November
Working day and night, receiving, sorting,
stacking parts.

Tuesday, 20 November
OFFENSIVE started, ground taken; guns going
like hell. Bridge loaded; 15 wagons of it ready
to move up tomorrow.

Wednesday, 21 November
Advance on right flank. Several villages taken,
centre and left holding. Coy. standing by,
Transport standing by.

Thursday, 22 November
Still advancing. Marcoing taken. Germans
holding on left and centre. In front of us a dozen
6" howitzers firing day and night, can observe
shells bursting along ridge ahead. Troops pouring
up; bridge transport still awaiting word to move
up.

Friday, 23 November

Guards Div. swung by today. Guns going back
and front of us. Germans shelling the village this
afternoon. Can see Bourlon Hill and wood in
front that is holding up our advance, and our
shells bursting on it and beyond. Coy. moved on
to Hermies last night. Am still left in charge of
bridge. Rations short, mostly bully and biscuits.
(In margin: **November 24th** Son born. *This was
William, who died in 1920.)* The thrust for
Cambrai fiercely contested. Villages changing
hands back and fore.

Sunday, 25 November

Cambrai battle still raging. Germans shelling this
village all day. Three men, eight horses killed in
barn near us. Our main roads under shellfire day
and night.

Friday, 30 November

Shelled from billet the last two nights. Sheltered
in old cellar. Fritz shells bursting along road and
each side billet. Started making dugout. Great
German counter-attack. They captured two Coys.
REs, Lab. Coy and S. Roller *(?)*, over 100 guns,
cut up 20th Div. badly.

Friday, 7 December

Had week making dugout. Last night German
'planes bombed village and they shelled us for two
hours. Could hear a number burst above us on
road. Men killed and wounded day and night in
village. Other day our Coy.Sgt.Major Bowers and
five men wounded by shell at HQ Hermies. Coy.
moved now to Ypres.

Monday, 10 December

Rumours of our retirement, after such terrible
sacrifices to gain here. Two bridges on main
Cambrai road recently built by 142 Coy. now
blown up. Germans retaking villages in the
Salient. German airmen busy over us here.
Anti-aircraft gun behind us blazing away off and
on all day; air duels common.

Friday, 14 December
Village shelled today, dropping around billet; we
dived for cover to dugout; South African
Artillery crowded in with us but their Major and a
Lieut. were killed on the road, a couple of yards
off. This 4.2 shell, a sort of ground shrapnel, is
terribly effective.

Saturday, 15 December
German 'planes raided and bombed this village at
dawn this morning. Our bridges being taken back
to Bapaume, the Cambrai thrust evidently a
FIASCO after all the joybells and press eulogy!!

Monday, 17 December
Shelled around billet four times today; first shell
bursting near means a flying dash to the dugout.
Was shaving this morning when, whizz–bang, a
shell landed in an old house near by. It's a sight
to see everyone dashing for his funk hole.
Germans blew up ammunition dump, Doignies,
next village.

Tuesday, 18 December
First snow. 3 in. getting up, snowing all day.

Friday, 21 December
Chased us into dugout twice yesterday evening
with shellfire. Country locked in snow and frost,
every tree, bush and leaf beautiful with white
frost crystals. Plenty of firing in these ruined
houses.

Monday, 24 December
Finished clearing bridges back to Bapaume.
Returned to Coy. HQ Thilloy, Christmas Eve,
about 10 miles. Freezing for a week now. Name
sent to Depot with 30 months O.S. *(Overseas
Service).* NCOs for substitution.

Tuesday, 25 December – Christmas Day
Very passable time. Gift of dozen bottles whisky
to sergeants from officers. Good dinner out of

canteen funds: pork, veg., Xmas pudd., then
champagne and beer. Smoker to wind up.
Address by C.O., etc.

Thursday, 27 December
With party building new 4th Corps HQ Grevillers.
Only pulled the damn place down three months
ago. 'Pop goes the weasel.'

Tuesday, New Year's Day
Fearful cold all day; looking after 150 Lab. and
General Service men on revetments.

Three years now in the Army, two years an
NCO, ten months a Sergeant. An interesting
year. Back area work in the summer, charge
of parties of coloured men, Germans, Colonials,
'Unfits' and alien Jews. Followed ANZAC
through Bapaume. Light Railways, etc. In
Cambrai Offensive and Retirement, with heavy
bridges.

Saturday, 5 January

Appointed Stove Inspector, all hut camps
Bapaume-Warlencourt area. Inspect and report if
recent GRO *(General Routine Order)* is complied
with ("piping to have 4 in. clearance").

Sunday, 6 January

Carbuncle on neck lanced by Yankee doctor; have
suffered considerably with this, but am still
carrying on; don't want to lose this job.

Thursday, 10 January

Had to forfeit my job. Going through hell three
times a day; doctor 'never saw a worse neck'. I
can believe him, for the squeezing and probing
process is pretty near the limit of endurance.
And the weather is vile, icy blizzards. One reads
and dozes over the stove 'tween times, but facing
any weather on works is preferable to this
periodic torture.

Monday, 14 January

Thaw set in, after a month of terribly hard frost
and snow. Flooded out of our tents now.

Sunday, 20 January

Had fourteen days ex-duty. Turn for leave
should be in about two weeks. Then am down for
substitution shortly. Depot should suit for spring
and summer, then, if another winter campaign,
must try for a move to the eastern hemisphere.
Camp Sgt. now, clearing up for moving. Spring
weather now.

Thursday, 24 January

Beaunatre. New camp. Company moved in today.

Friday, 25 January

Attending Field Ambulance 25th Div. This is
fourth doctor during three weeks. Started
fomentations again.

Tuesday, 29 January

Bombed by German 'planes these last two nights

owing to full moon. Last evening he had a fine raid, our searchlights sweeping the sky, several anti-aircraft guns banging away and the rattle of machine guns sweeping. We had to take shelter in a trench dug in the camp for that purpose. He dropped one in some horse lines near, destroying 80 horses, 45 killed outright. Also bombed CCS Achiet-le-Grand, killed several nurses, wounded a lot of patients.

Thursday, 31 January
Away on leave again. Bombing raids the last four nights. Leaving Bapaume 7.30 this evening.

Friday, 1 February
All night journey to Boulogne, fearfully cold journey. Detained all day in rest billet, 'standing by' all the time. Crossed Channel 4.30, London 10 p.m. Put up Sal*(vation)* Army Soldiers' Rest.

Friday, 8 February
Evening to Cheltenham. Visited aeroplane factory. Dad working there. (Got Credit from Chatham £20. Put £33 away.)

Monday, 11 February
Visited brother Newport. [*This was Newport in Gwent and the brother was Charles Fisher, the father of the present editor.*] Altogether a good 14 days' holiday.

Friday, 15 February
Returned to France.

Saturday, 16 February
Reached Coy.

Monday, 18 February
Job at Bihucourt. Hut camp; our men on task work. 90 Mongolian labourers excavating foundations; strong chaps, very intelligent. Tenpence a day pay. No pay if daily ticket not signed. German air raid again at night, bombs

dropped close to huts, door perforated with splinters; near thing.

Tuesday, 19 February
Job at Morshies. New corps defence line of trenches. Fine system of trenches in case of the great German thrust coming this way. Fine stretch of landscape, lovely weather, Lagnicourt in front, then Queant.

Saturday, 23 February
Germans shelling this new line, also the batteries behind.

Sunday, 24 February
Long-range gun again. Fresnicourt (parallel with us) shelled. Also Vaux (in front of us) getting it hot. Clouds of smoke rising continually from the ruined villages.

Monday, 25 February
New trench shelled today, a regular bombardment, shells landing just short and beyond; traverses blown in. Party had to clear away to safety. Complete collapse of Russia, accept German terms.

Tuesday, 5 March
Weather last month fine, every indication of spring. Now cold blizzards, mud, snow. Last month quartermaster and corporal substituted. Now three more sergeants relieved. Will miss these sergeants after associating for three years.

Thursday, 7 March
Took over detachment at Vaux, 18 of our chaps, attached to detachment of 252nd Tunnelling Company. On deep dugouts in Corps R Lines, billeting in old farm stable, 8 hours on, 24 hours off, not bad at all. Am just here for discipline, don't need to go on works.

Sunday, 10 March
Beautiful weather, sun all day, as warm as

summer. Every night expecting Jerry to attack. We have to report with our detachments to Brigade HQ in case of German attack. Taste of mustard gas early yesterday morning.

Monday, 11 March

Village shelled today, evidently after these 12-inch guns. First shell landed in billet other side this farmyard; luckily men (Shropshires) away for bath. Shells each side and beyond billet. Men have to wear respirators hour a day now.

Wednesday, 13 March

Yesterday evening everyone in a fever of excitement about a German attack this morning. All troops standing to in the reserve trenches. We had to report at 5.0 a.m. Terrific bombardment all night. We "fell in" and marched away in the dark and watched the dawn from corps line, but no Fritz. We observed a squad of our 'planes bomb an ammunition dump.

Sunday, 17 March

St. Patrick's Day, summer weather. Twelve months a sergeant tomorrow. Taking Tunnellers and our chaps each day for an hour's gas drill. Lounging in the sunshine, facing the old ruined church; beside it a French cemetery, crosses, shrines and vaults, many torn up or smashed by shell fire. Next a group of ANZAC graves, then again a large German cemetery. Overhead the soaring singing lark and the hum of our aerial patrols. And at regular intervals the crash of our heavy guns behind the village and the more frequent bang bang of our field guns to the left of us. I suppose this is shortly to finish for me, a few weeks and I am on substitution, then off goes my acting rank if I don't manage to get confirmed in the meantime.

Wednesday, 20 March

Interview Major Coates, our C.O. He is trying to get us substantiated rank.

Thursday, 21 March

Big German attack commences. At 5.0 a.m. we were roused by a furious shelling, the village alive with bursting shells; some gas shells. Coughing and choking we slipped on masks; noise was terrific and it was dark too. We cleared out from village, dodging the shells and collected party together on the plain. Unable to return to billet we retired to Rancourt, HQ 252nd Tunnelling Company; had to take cover crossing the plain. We have lost our equipment and rifles, but were lucky to get away ourselves. Party later in the day failed to get into Vaux; another detachment of our Coy. in from Bometz. Capt. Holland wounded, others safe. Evening, party returned to our HQ. Had to give report of how we lost equipment. 8.30 out with party marking out trench for brigade. Return before midnight, battle still raging. Germans take Vaux, advance four miles.

Friday, 22 March

Germans still attacking. Hasty 'fall in' marching order, with shovel, shells bursting in camp, and around us on parade. We retire away on slight ridge and strip off, and men are digging themselves in as I write. Batteries retiring are taking up positions about here. Jerry is shelling road behind us towards Bapaume, a field ambulance and number of camps. German advance eight miles.

Saturday, 23 March

Yesterday evening front of Mory, digging trench after dark, we had lost our positions ahead; our inf (antry) holding advanced machine-gun posts in front of us. Digging like hell, expecting him to attack, should have had to man fire-step. Bullets singing over us, our field guns behind us blazing away from open positions. Away before dawn, marched back to Bihucourt, tem (porary) billet in old Suchery, thoroughly worn out. Germans slowly advancing, company parading full marching

order before dinner. Marching away back to
Bucquoy, hot day. Civilians evac *(uated)*, out again
evening, lorry back to Bihucourt. Marched to
Biefvillers, digging trenches behind Bapaume with
labour companies. German advance ten miles.

Sunday, 24 March

Thoroughly dead beat. Evening, out with 300 of
150th labour company. Trenching again in front
Bihucourt. Villages ahead of us undergoing
bombardment, wounded coming back say Jerry
still advancing. Have a job to keep these lab *(our)*
chaps to finish trench, owing to shelling. German
shells going over us into Bihucourt. Returned
before midnight, billet shelled. Hasty pack up;
marched away back to Bucquoy. Roads congested
with retiring troops and transport. Germans take
Bihucourt. Total advance 15 miles.

Monday, 25 March

Arrived Bucquoy after three hours. Advance
party with tea ready; a rough kip. 10.0 a.m.
fall in again, marched back to Serre through old
Somme battle-torn area. Resting here, dinner,
transport pouring past us in retreat. Away again,
crossing the original British front-line trench
before Somme off *(ensive)*, the old Suchery.
Arrived Mailly, billeted here, tea, civilians here,
cafés open, had some wine. But people to clear
out in 24 hours. Total German advance 18 miles.

Tuesday, 26 March

Hasty pack up again, and off again. Germans in
next village. Sergeants made responsible for own
sections. Poisoned hand aching, foot raw, but
want to stick this stunt through. Bertrancourt,
stayed for dinner, off again through Buss,
Louvencourt. Halted Rainchval for the night.
Germans take Bapaume and Péronne.

Wednesday, 27 March

Rainchval. Jerry was here bombing last night,
shells dropping here this morning. Up and

marched away by seven o'clock through Marieux,
Threves to Pas-en-Artois. About 10 miles;
beautiful wooded hills. Civilians packing and
moving. Company billeted here at Pas-en-Artois.
Starting work on new line of defence. Germans
take Albert.

Thursday, 28 March

Hand very bad, sick with it. Lorry to Doullens,
about eight miles. Admitted 3rd Canadian
Hospital (poisoned hand), crowds of wounded
pouring in. Asked doctor to lance my hand to
avoid going down line, but he says, "No facilities
here." Awaiting evacuation, wards crowded,
everyone dead beat, just throw themselves down
in their dirty clothes, bloody bandages. Raining
now, to add to the misery.

Friday, 29 March – Good Friday

Doullens. Still awaiting evacuation. Just turned
dinner we boarded ambulance cars for railway
station. While there King George and staff came
along hospital train. Seems a decent, unassuming
chap. Comfortable riding, good meals served,
good book.

Saturday, 30 March

Travelling all night, breakfast. Taken to Rouen 12
General Hospital. Some marked England, the
others for convalescent camp. I am for operating
theatre. Evening turn for the theatre; too
ghastly business-looking. Boots removed, lie on
table; I enquire of surgeon: "Can't I avoid the
chloroform?" "Can you stand pain?" "Better
than chloroform." "Right!" My hand is opened;
blood flows, fomented, away to bed.

Sunday, 31 March

My card marked Blighty, hand still rather bad.

Monday, 1 April

2.0 a.m. roused and away in cars for station.
Train journey to Le Havre. Cold ride. Embarked

12 o'clock boat (ordinary). Draft of men from
Salonica on board. Biscuits, bully, cheese at 2
o'clock (first since yesterday). Seasick for the
first time in eight cross–channel trips.
Southampton at 6.30 p.m. Reached Manchester
4.30 a.m.

Tuesday, 2 April

Stockport, Lancs. By taxi to Manchester. 2nd
Western General Hospital. Hollywood Park
School, about 120 beds. Hand rapidly mending,
confined to bed, best of feeding. Nurses nice
girls.

Sunday, 7 April

Hand nearly well. Get out any afternoon, hospital
blue, overcoat. Picture–house or library,
concerts. Food here very good, plenty of books.
Expecting to be marked 'Away' any day.

Friday, 12 April

Discharged from hospital 'fit for duty'. Home for
four days' leave. Hand still a little stiff and sore.
Expected a spell at convalescent camp. Don't
mind how soon I'm out again now; can't fancy
soldiering at home depots.

Tuesday, 16 April

Leave up, but no travel warrant. Reported C.O.
Troops, Birmingham. 'Must wait for warrant.'
Rather want to get across again. Belgium/French
frontier offensive assuming serious proportions.

Friday, 19 April

Travel warrant from Chatham. Leave extended to
the 21st (10 days). To report 5th Reserve
Battalion, RE, Christchurch, Hants.

Saturday, 20 April

Half-day Cheltenham, lost last train but caught
empty return.

Sunday, 21 April
Away to Christchurch, fearful day, snow and rain,
bitter cold. Reached destination 10.30.

Monday, 22 April
Christchurch, Hants. Sent to H Coy., the Draft
Coy. Usual thing, men returning from hospital,
even fit, to be marked A3 and worked up through
the different companies to this one. But owing to
circumstances I am A1; so expect a short stay
here. Very fine locality this; everyone passed
through physical training to fit them. I miss
this, which suits me.

Tuesday, 23 April
MO's Inspection. 'Hand right, Sergeant?' 'Yes,
sir.' FIT. Down for draft tomorrow, owing to
men not having turned up from leave. This is
record move for this place. But it just happens
to suit me.

Saturday, 27 April
From Southampton 6.30. Sailed this evening,
lovely weather. Draft of 85. Am only sergeant.
An officer as conducting party. This is 9th
cross-channel journey.

Sunday, 28 April
Arrive Le Havre 12.30. 18-hour trip. Marched
rest camp 3 miles, eggs and sausage dinner.
Paraded and marched docks, then back again,
pouring rain. Rest camp for night.

Monday, 29 April
Reveille 5 o'clock, parade 7 o'clock for docks.
Some job this, 85 men to look after: rations,
blankets, sudden parades, the men naturally none
too sweet on returning. Arrived Rouen, RE Base
Depot.

Wednesday, 1 May
Two days drawing equipment, etc., MO inspection,
CO inspection, gas tested; and the important

interview with adjutant who drops acting ranks.
Severe cross-examination. He has allowed me to
retain sergeant's rank. This Base very extensive
now, extremely regimental. Hot on NCOs.
Sergeants and corporals go through squad drill
under instructors, also musketry and field works,
physical drill, gas drill.

Saturday, 4 May
On musketry. Won sweepstake shooting.

Monday, 13 May
Sick, boil on neck. MO. Been here two weeks,
training all over again. Infantry drill, musketry,
gas, bayonet, physical. Not unnecessary for us
NCOs who were rushed out with little training; a
bit of a bore, though.

Wednesday, 15 May
With party of NCOs, full marching order, away to
Rouen, to report to CRE. Stayed night in town;
some job tomorrow. Glorious weather, but hot
for marching with equipment. Three years today
I landed in France.

Thursday, 16 May
Sent to Deville, Rouen suburb, 5th HRS, MT,
ASC. Big repair workshops, concrete and girders.
German prisoner labour. Rush job. Pretty
village, lying in wooded valley. Like a couple of
weeks here; real good mess.

Sunday, 26 May
Look like having spell here, work under the best
conditions I've had yet. We attached RE
sergeants do not parade. Good roomy hut, best
mess yet, also late pass. City one side; ideal
country walks the other.

Sunday, 16 June
Good variety of work. Concrete foundations for
huge repair shed. On bridge now, concrete
pillars. German prisoners take much super-
vision.

Sunday, 23 June
German 'planes over Rouen, bombing, number of casualties.

Sunday, 30 June
Job raising and levelling floors with chalk; dispose 120 skips each day. Chinese labour, stubborn fellows to handle.

Sunday, 14 July
Here over two months now: hours 7 - 5.30, no parades for us REs; any time night; cinema last night, Rouen; every Sunday off. Sweating on a recall to depot any time.

Sunday, 21 July
Returned to base depot yesterday. Recalled for draft. Made an evening of it in Maromme with a few friends. Vermouth-cassis. Reached depot this morning soaked to the skin; expected trouble but just missed it. Warned today for 554 Coy.

Tuesday, 23 July
Started away for up the line, 45 of us, odds and ends for different Coys. 30-odd in rail van, lying across each other.

Wednesday, 24 July
Reached Coy. 554 Army Troops (F.F.) Le Nieppe, pretty village, few miles from St. Omer. This is a Dundee Territorial Coy, been out three years on good jobs. Am a bit apprehensive. But after all it matters little how things go. Interview with C.O. not very promising. Is sending to Records for my sub *(stantive)* rank. *(In margin:* VII Corps)

Friday, 26 July
Coy. moved to Longnesse (St. Omer) constructing new defence line. Chink labour. Billet old farm; half-mile into town.

Monday, 29 July
Out with C.O., surveying and marking out

trenches, through cornfields, potatoes, etc.,
meaning cutting path 21 ft. wide through these
fine crops.

Thursday, 1 August

Beautiful country round St. Omer. Interesting
job, about the hills all day, overlooking the old
town. Evenings the town is alive with English,
Chinks, Yanks, Australians; the cafés crowded,
singing and drinking Tommies; licensed brothel.
Every fine night, bombing raids over here.

Friday, 16 August

Return arrived from Records. Chat. Was made
Substantive Sergeant, 18.4.18. Things running
very smooth now, a decent lot of chaps; a good
mess, Poker the game. Still scouting around the
hills, marking trenches.

Monday, 19 August

Off to Escoulles, 2nd Army Gas School. A fine
16-mile run top of motor bus.

Tuesday, 27 August

Returned after a week's gas course. A stiff time,
15 lectures, a big subject. Gas NCO important
position in every unit; nature of enemy gases,
method of using; treatment of gas casualties;
protection of billets, gas-proofing; exactness of
gas drill; recording of attacks. Awaiting result
of exam. PASSED: 'Very Good. A very keen
student.'

Friday, 30 August

Taken over wiring job, St. Omer defence line.
Chink labour, task work.

Tuesday, 10 September

Away to Caestre, a village smashed up by Jerry's
recent offensive. Refugees drifting back here.
Under canvas, weather bad, rained every day this
month. Coy. to throw bridges over the Lys.

Wednesday, 11 September

By lorry each day to Bailleul. Unloading heavy bridges; making 2nd Army B Dump. Germans recently evacuated this town, all smashed up. Passing through Flette and Wetteren, retaken by us lately. This big railway siding, shelled off and on most nights.

Saturday, 21 September

Still sorting and stacking bridges. South African nigger labour, good workers if interested in job. Am laying light railway.

Wednesday, 25 September

Away for day's course – Etaples. Heavy pontoon bridging; 20-mile lorry trip.
Bulgaria given in.

Thursday, 10 October

Away on detachment (Nieppe). Building heavy iron bridge over River Lys, just outside Armentières. Jerry blew up old one on retirement. This is 90-ton 'Hopkins'. Last week Jerry pushed from Armentières. Billet in cellar beneath ruined villa, between batteries. Through the night Germans shell the village, already in ruins.

Thursday, 17 October

Launched Armentières bridge, first heavy bridge of the 2nd Army. 150 ft. long, 90 tons; Germans had blown buttress out.

Friday, 18 October

Off to heavy bridging school. Party of 15 for three weeks' course. Train to Etaples; night in No. 9 Rest Camp.

Saturday, 19 October

Train to Anvin, marched to Monchy Cayse. Everybody excited about the War finishing soon.

Sunday, 20 October

Course started, hours 8 – 4. Most of us NCOs;

all of us work, very heavy job. Lectures and
practical bridge-building. Only bridging school on
Western Front. REs, mostly NCOs, Australians,
Canadians, tunnellers, etc., from all the way
through Belgium and France. Sgts.' Mess
providing interesting discussions.

Thursday, 31 October
Turkey finished. "Unconditional surrender."
Hard work, dirty jobs, swampy ground.
(Line illegible.)

Friday, 8 November
Last day of course. All very glad, what with
rain, mud, heavy slogging, working out bridge
reconnaissance schemes. My squad 'J' got highest
marks in school. I got highest marks, 180 out of
200, for my reconnaissance scheme. But didn't
get on well with the staff.

Saturday, 9 November
Started by train away to company via Etaples,
Boulogne, St. Omer. Night in Etaples rest camp,
everyone excited.

Sunday, 10 November
All day travelling: Boulogne, Calais, St. Omer,
Bailleul, the devastated belt, on past
Passchendaele, Menin, then in the dark railhead
Courtrai, something up. As we alighted, a hell of
a noise - fireworks. WAR FINISHED! Everyone
mad with joy, processions, Belgian civilians, men,
women, British and Colonials, arm-in-arm,
singing, shouting, trumpets, tin cans, huge bonfire
Central Square, thousands dancing. We stayed in
big hotel the night.

Monday, 11 November
Arrived Coy. village Heule outside Courtrai, army
bridging dump. HOSTILITIES ENDED;
COLLAPSE OF GERMANY.

Sunday, 17 November
Our Coy. charge bridging dump, receiving and

dispatching bridges, for River Schelt. Alien
Jewish labour coy. One topic of conversation now
- demobilization.

Sunday, 1 December
C.O. gone hospital - 'flu. Coy. every other day
off, Courtrai busy town, plenty of life, cinemas,
concerts, drinks very dear.

Sunday, 15 December
As treasurer and secretary of Sgts.' Mess away
with lorry to St. Omer to get stuff of Xmas
dinner. Took £20 with me. Travelled via
Courtrai, Roubaix, Lille, Armentières, Hazebrouck.
Everything extra dear, fowls, hares, beer, wine,
fruit. Took three days, had a good time. On
return got orders to leave the following day on
detachment. Filled up demobilization form.

Tuesday, 17 December
Away to Menin. Charge of party of 20.
Attached 214 AT Coy. Rebuilding light railway
bridge over River Lys. Salvaging piles and timber
from Jerry dumps.

Wednesday, 25 December - Christmas Day
Detachment called in for annual dinner. Quite a
good thing, plenty of everything. Smoker after
till midnight.

Sunday, 29 December
Agreed to be Cadre Sergeant, one of 26 left
behind to hand over the coy. stores and
equipment after demobilization.

Tuesday, 31 December - New Year's Eve
Called in to HQ NCOs Dinner & Smoker. A great
time.

Four years in the Army. War finished. Caught
in the rush of the German spring offensive and
the retirement, then hospital and Blighty, the
quick return, two months' base work. Sent to
Dundee AT Coy., summer on defence work, gas
school and bridging school. Passed out. On the
big Armentières bridge. Then finishing the year
on a railway pile bridge at Menin for the 214 RE
Coy.

Friday, 10 January
Took over Sgt. in charge bridging dump and
stores. 5th Army bridging dump. Fair job.
Issuing heavy bridge and stores. Cape Coloured
labour on dump.

Tuesday, 28 January
Sgt.Major away on leave. Am Acting Coy.
Sgt.Major in his absence. Fairly busy job, men
coming and going, leave, demobilized,
detachments, schools of inst *(?ruction)*. Am also
treasurer of coy. canteen.

Thursday, 13 February
Terrible accident early this morning. At 3.0 a.m.
wakened by guard; cobbler's hut on fire, rushed
out to find hut a blazing furnace, impossible to do
anything for him; job to prevent other huts from
firing.

Friday, 14 February
Board of enquiry, two days. Had to explain why
I could not save him. One realised the respon-
sibilities of a CSM. Sgt.Major returned off leave
and away again, 'Demob.' C.O. promises to ask
CRE to make me CSM.

Saturday, 1 March

Practically down to Cadre. Just keeping things moving. Thinking of signing on for another year, Army of Occupation. Garrison duty in *(illegible)* looks good.

Saturday, 15 March

Signed on for another year in Army of Occupation; tossed for it.

Monday, 17 March

Birthday. Lorry trip to Ostend. Grand pleasure resort before the war. All signs of recent occupation; concrete fortress defences, hotels on sea front much damaged. Saw the *Vindictive*, mouth of harbour. Had a good day, discovered some Scotch whisky.

Wednesday, 19 March

Moving order to 167 AT Coy, 14 Div. Roncq, France. On water supply. CSM about to be demobilized; rumour that I am taking over. Am not keen. This Coy. being made up of *(uncertain reading)*.

Saturday, 22 March

Away on leave, via Calais.

Sunday, 23 March

Crossed over. Birmingham same evening.

Saturday, 5 April

Midnight. Returning from Birmingham.

Sunday, 6 April

Left Shorncliffe for Calais.

Monday, 7 April

Reached Coy. late evening, Roncq.

Tuesday, 8 April

Took over Acting CSM, 167 AT Coy, 70 strong; things very quiet.

Sunday, 13 April
Joy ride sidecar, Roubaix. Football, British versus French. Finish up vin blanc. Good day.

Thursday, 17 April
Coy. moving Reninghelst. Self moved down with reinforcements.
.

Friday, 18 April – Good Friday
Reninghelst, building camp. Coy. on water system, supplying Chinese and POW camps. Rest of Coy. moved Reninghelst with new C.O. Capt. McFail.

Friday, 2 May
Promoted COY.SGT.MAJOR. The top of the tree. Glorious weather. Camp on ridge. View of Mt. Kemmel. Not altogether keen about this rank. A lot of responsibility for little extra remuneration. Pay now:

	s.	d.
Regular	1	2
Trade	1	4
Rank	2	7
War		4
Bonus	2	6
Field Allowance		6
Gratuity		4

8s. 9d. a day

Friday, 6 June
Slight haemorrhage through the day. So the little beggars have overtaken me again. Oh well! San Nefer Rean . . . .

* * * * * * * * * * * * *

Editorial Note:

This version of 'San Fairy Ann', i.e. 'Ça ne fait rien', ends the diary.

It is perhaps typical that this last word should be on an indifferent note: "Oh, well – it doesn't matter."

Army records show that Will's BEF service ended on 20 July and that in March 1920 he was discharged A1 (which seems highly questionable) on completion of engagement.

In June 1919 his fourth son William (born in 1917 – see diary entry of 23 November) died. In November 1920 a second daughter was born; this was Emily and she survived until her seventieth year. Of his six children only Sydney now survives, but there are grandchildren in Britain and in the States.

Will himself died at the end of July 1922, in hospital in Birmingham. He was then forty and he died of tuberculosis, the disease which started in the Welsh coalmines and plagued him throughout his Army career.

APPENDIX I

The final pages of the diary/notebook contain the following list of books. His constant references in the diary to "a good read" must certainly refer to some of these. The asterisks are his and may well indicate favourites.

?	Short-Lived Bushrangers
Baring-Gould, S.	Eve
Le Gallienne, R.	The Quest for the Golden Girl *
Ward, Mrs. Humphry	Canadian Born
Cross, Victoria	Five Knights
Sutro, Alfred	Foolish Virgins
Cullum, Ridgeworth	The Compact
Vachell, H.A.	John Charity
Orczy, Baroness	Beau Brocade
" "	Petticoat Government
Hornung, E.W.	A Bride from the Bush
?	The World Masters
Balot *(?)*, Alphonse	The Woman of Fire
McCulloch, David	The Swinging Tub *
Wile, F.W.M.	The Assault
Lancaster, G.B.	A Spur to Smile
Holland, Clive	My Japanese Wife
Grant, James	The Phantom Regiment
Ballantyne, R.M.	Ungava
London, Jack	The Iron Heel *
Thurston, Temple	Sally Bishop
Irvine, Alex	My Lady of the Chimney Corner *
Phillpotts, Eden	Virgin in Judgement *
Henry, O.	The Gentle Grafter
Crawford, M.	Paul Petoff
Henry, O.	The Four Million
London, Jack	Smoke Below
Bronson, Ed. B.	Reminiscences of a Ranchman ***

Wells, H.G.	Ann Veronica *
Schreiner, Olive	The Story of an African Farm **
Dell, Ethel M.	The Knave of Diamonds
Wilde, Oscar	The Picture of Dorian Gray
Hornung, E.W.	A Thief in the Night
Lawless, Hon. Emily	Hurish
Bancroft, F.	The Veldt Dwellers
Page, Gertrude	The Pathway
Weyman, Stanley J.	The Abbess of May
Boothby, Guy	Love Made Manifest
" "	Beautiful White Devil
Orczy, Baroness	Eldorado
Page, Gertrude	Follow After
Balfour, Andrew	To Arms
Anonymous	Me
London, Jack	Adventure
Gibbon, Percival	(?) Grobelar's Cases
Ibanez, Vicente Blasco	The Matador (translated from the Spanish by Mrs. Gillespie)
Oppenheim, E.P.	False Evidence
Page, Gertrude	The Rhodesian
Le Queux, William	The Catspaw
Oppenheim, E.P.	The Lost Leader
Willard, Dolf	The Story of Eden
Stratton-Porter, Gene	Freckles
Curwood, James O.	Phil Steel N.W.M.P.
Oppenheim, E.P.	Havoc
?	Roar of the Sea
Oppenheim, E.P.	The World's Great Snare *
Russell, W. Clark	My Danish Sweetheart
Orczy, Baroness	Old Man in the Corner
Merriman, H. Seton	Slave of the Lamp
Buchan, John	The Power House
Rita (?)	The House Opposite
Webster, Jean	Jerry
Stratton-Porter, Gene	The Harvester *
Haggard, Rider	Nada the Lily
Marchmont, A.W.	Under the Black Eagle

Stratton-Porter, Gene	A Girl of the Limberlost
Maxwell, W.B.	Hill Rise *
Willard, Dolf	Unofficial Honeymoon
Raine, Allan	A Welsh Singer
Payn, James	The Burnt Million
Doyle, A. Conan	Uncle Bernac
London, Jack	Tales of the Fish Patrol
Orczy, Baroness	Fire in Stubble
Raine, Allan	Torn Sails
Pemberton, Max	Mystery of the Green Heart
Merriman, H. Seton	One Generation to Another
Macdonald, J.M.	Thunderbolt *
Le Queux, William	In White Raiment
Broome, H.A.	Log of a Rolling Stone
Croker, B.M.	The Happy Valley
Oppenheim, E.P.	Jenny of the Marshes
Marsh, Richard	The Beatle
Stratton-Porter, Gene	Laddie
Le Queux, William	Wiles of the Wicked
Doyle, A. Conan	The Valley of Fear
Williams, Captain G.	In the Hands of the Senoussi
Stratton-Porter, Gene	The Foot of the Rainbow
Hay, Ian	A Knight on Wheels
?	Nana's Daughter
Birmingham, George	The Lost Tribes
Pemberton, Max	Pro Patria
Forman, Justice M.	The Garden of Iris
Belloc, Hilaire	The Great European War (First Phase)
Locke, William	The White Dove
Hewlett, Maurice	The Forest Lovers
Vachell, H.A.	The Face of Clay
Stacpoole, H. de Vere	Patsy *
Clauston, Storer	A Lunatic at Large
Mason, A.E.W.	The Watchers
Robins, Elizabeth	The Magnetic North *
Oppenheim, E.P.	An Illustrious Prince
Turgenev, Ivan	Nest of Hereditary Legislators *
O'Brien, E.J. (Ed.)	Best Short Stories (US) 1915

Cross, Victoria	The Life Sentence
Le blanc, Maurice	Arsène Lupin
Mason, A.E.W.	The Philanderers
Becke, Luis	By Reef and Palm
London, Jack	A Son of the Sun
White, Stewart E.	The River Man *
Morrison, Arthur	A Child of the Jago *
Thurston, Katherine	Max
Page, Gertrude	The Edge o' the Beyond *
Haggard, Rider	Queen Sheba's Ring
Vachell, H.A.	Brothers *
Smart, Hawley	A Daughter of Vanity
Locke, William	At the Gate of Somaria *
White, Stewart Ed.	The Blazed Trail *
Stacpoole, H. de Vere	Cpl. Jacques of the Foreign Legion
White, Stewart Ed.	The Westerners *
Stevenson, R.L.	New Arabian Nights
Westcott, Ed. Noyes	David Harum
Dehan, Richard	The Man of Iron *
Henry, O.	The Trimmed Lamp *
Stephens, G.M.	With Kitchener to Khartoum
Henry, O.	Heart of the West
Galon, Tom	Cometkeep
Blatchford, R.	God and My Neighbour
Becke, Louis	Bully Hayes Buccaneer
Haels, A.J.	McCluskey the Reformer *
Beach, Rex	The Iron Trail
Pocock, Roger	A Frontiersman *
Graves, Dr. A.K.	Secrets German War Office
Street, Dr. M.	*(Title uncertain).*

APPENDIX II

Page 78 of the diary/notebook contains this analysis of the degeneration of the human race. As we have already seen, Will was no optimist!

Mothers, in overdrawing on their constitutional reserves to enable them to do men's work, exhaust the constitutional resources of the generation to come. Naturally a woman is less strong in body and brain than man is because a far greater proportion of her vital power is invested in her for possible motherhood. When women are trained to compete physically, professionally and industrially with men, this natural investment in them of vital power for racial purposes is prevented and the race suffers proportionally. The increasing strain, educational and industrial, which has been put of late years on our developing girls and young women has entailed an alarming increase of national defect and degeneracy. And because inheritance is from father to daughter and from mother to son this alarming increase of disease and defect has wreaked itself more on the boys than girls. When women develop masculine physique and brains they do so directly at the cost of the brains and physique of possible sons. So the mortality of male infants, particularly, has increased of late. In 1860 only 91 more boys died than girls. In 1913 this excess in mortality of boys leapt to 33 per cent. This diminished vital power of male infants begins before birth, 180 boys being born prematurely as compared with 145 girls. Of boys born, 7 die from inborn defects to 6. Before 3 months old four boys die to 3 girls. Of 1,000 infants 96 girls die before a year old as compared to 120 boys. Strenuous women (golf, tennis, hockey) have more girls; the boys usually physically and mentally below average.

APPENDIX III

*These tables form part of Page 79 of the notebook.
They give another insight into the way Will's mind
was working.*

| Waterloo | 8 hours | 3 mile front |
| B Force | 23,000 | B Cas. 8,300 |

| Ypres | 15 days | 30 mile front |
| B Force | 120,000 | B Cas. 50,000 |

| Crimea | 1,855 | |
| B Force | 33,000 | |

	£.
Annual Income GB	2,300,000,000
Annual Expenditure GB	2,000,000,000
Annual Savings and Investments GB	350,000,000
Value of our Foreign Investments	4,000,000,000
Daily Revenue from Taxation	750,000
We spent on Napoleonic Wars	800,000,000
which works out at less per week than	1,000,000
Present War costing us per year	1,000,000,000
First 5 months this year - Imports ?	32,000,000
While our Ex- and Re-Exports ?	73,750,000
For 12 months our Indebtedness	260,000,000

Obituaries of Lieutenant George Fisher, Will's brother, who died on 20 December 1916 from war wounds:

"GLOUCESTERSHIRE ECHO", 27 December 1916
Casualties to Local Officers
Lieut. Geo. Fisher

Many old friends of Lieut. Geo. Fisher, son of Mr. Charles Fisher of 34 Swindon Road, Cheltenham (who has long been connected with the Cheltenham Trades and Labour Council, Cheltenham Education Committee, and other bodies in the town), will hear with great regret of his death at a private hospital, 50 Weymouth Street, London, from wounds received in action. Lieut. Fisher was sent back to England on Saturday week with two bullet wounds in the abdomen, and during last week his father received from him a cheerful note stating that he was going on very well. He went through the necessary operation satisfactorily, but later his condition became worse. Being advised of this his father hurried up to London, only to arrive two hours after his son had passed away. The dead officer at one time held a position in the employ of the Gloucester Co-operative Society in Cheltenham; and some of his old friends will also remember him as a member of the elocution class run some years ago in connection with the Trades and Labour Council Evening School in Grosvenor Street. An earnest young fellow with a strong Socialistic trend, his friends regarded him as representing the higher aspirations of that movement, and also respected him

for his keen literary enthusiasm. About five or six
years ago he emigrated to Canada, where for some
years he was at Eaton's, the Canadian "Whiteley's".
Early in the war he gave up a good position to join
the Canadian forces, and after training in England
went to the front over 12 months ago. He was for
some time engaged in duties at the base but,
wishing to serve in the fighting line, he applied for
transfer, and was granted this with a commission, he
having previously been a sergeant. He was wounded
upon his first period of service at the front.

"GLOUCESTERSHIRE ECHO", 28 December 1916
Casualties to Local Officers
Lieut. G. Fisher: An Appreciation

Mr. Ed. J. Burrow writes:

I was shocked to see in your last night's issue the
report of poor George Fisher's death in hospital.
Up to the time of his being bowled over by the
wounds that eventually proved fatal, we were in close
touch with one another by correspondence; and it
was one of the pleasures of this drear war period to
be of assistance to him with a record of character
gleaned from personal knowledge when Geo. Fisher
was applying for his lieutenant's commission.
George Fisher was one of my old Salem Institute
boys - a fascinating character, with a weird mixture
of commonsense and idealism in his mental make-up.
Always irksome of the restrictions and bonds of
civilisation as he saw it, he, like many other of my
friends at the Institute, broke the chains of his
commonplace fate and set his face towards the
Eldorado of the West, where a man is appraised

more nearly at his native worth. He was, I know, on the way to good fortune when the call of the Mother Country spoke straightway to the idealist and the poet in George Fisher's soul; he was the last man to take up arms against brother-man had he not been sure of the Righteousness of the Cause he embraced. But George Fisher never thought twice when he saw the Gleam; and, after much training and promotion to sergeant's rank, and, later, a lieutenant's commission, I heard from him in France, thinking not of his own discomforts, but scheming out the details of a Maple-Leaf Christmas Card, which he wanted me to produce for him. This card was to go from all the officers of the regiment to their friends in Canada as a token of regard and well-being. And, alas! the news will flash over the wires that a line must be drawn through one of those names when the card reaches its destination. For George Fisher, the boy and man we knew and got to love so well, has paid the last debt to the country that bore him. But he will live in our memories; and when the battle flags are furled and we count up the men from Salem Institute who have given their lives for their country, we shall find the name of George Fisher very high up the list as a worthy representative of the high traditions of the comrades of those happy years we spent together at the old place.

(Mr. Burrow was a writer, illustrator and publisher under his own name. At one time he was Chairman of the Cheltenham Chamber of Commerce.)

APPENDIX V

An obituary of Charles Fisher, Will's father, published in the Gloucestershire Echo *on Thursday, 6 November 1924.*

DEATH OF A CHELTENHAM LABOUR LEADER

A host of his fellow craftsmen and of those interested in the trade union movement, as well as many townspeople who knew him in other capacities, will learn with regret of the death of Mr. Charles Fisher of 34 Swindon Street, the veteran Cheltenham Labour leader, which took place on Sunday, at the age of 77 years.

A mason by trade, Mr. Fisher had for 55 years been a member of the Bricklayers' Union. He was the first president of the Cheltenham Trade and Labour Council, and continued in that office from 1894 to 1899, he having been one of the founders of the organisation. In his capacity as president of the Council, in the days before the paid agents of the unions figured so largely in trade disputes, he generally figured as a representative of the men in local trade disputes, and as such, we believe, he won much respect from the employers. For although an earnest advocate of I.L.P. Socialism, and the bettering of the condition of his own class, and a man to be relied on by his people, he belonged to a type that could give reasons and see reason.

He was a prominent member of the now extinct Cheltenham Working Men's Institute, he being one of the now rather old-fashioned type who were as keen on qualifying the working man to occupy a better social position as the modern soap-box agitator is to pull down everybody who chances to have reached it.

In 1920 *(? 1902)* Mr. Fisher, as a Labour candidate, ran for the Town Council at a South Ward election, but was defeated by Mr. T.E. Rickerby (C) by 620 votes to 280. In the following year, however, he was paid the compliment of being selected as one of the first co-opted members of the Cheltenham Education Committee, which dates from that year. On it he found congenial occupation, and he remained a member several years. He represented the working classes well, but proved himself something better than a mere partisan of one class, for it was evident to anyone attending the meetings that he was one who had at heart the interests of education for its own sake. In 1908 he was given a place on the Pensions Committee by the Town Council, and in the same year he carried in the Education Committee an amendment respecting contractors who did not pay fair wages. We believe Mr. Fisher sat on the Education Committee until 1910, and we know that his fellow members bade goodbye to this keen old educationist not without regret.

The war brought bereavement to Mr. Fisher by the loss of a son who had emigrated to Canada, and who fell in France, where he had served as an officer in the Canadian Army.

The funeral took place on Thursday afternoon, there being present at the graveside a number of old comrades of the trade union organisations with which during life the deceased was connected. Amongst those present were: Mr. J. Betteridge, J.P. (representing Building Trades Federation), Mr. H. Addis (secretary of the Amalgamated Union of Building Trade Workers), Mr. J. Carr, J.P., and Mr. A.E. South (president and secretary of the Cheltenham and District Trades and Labour Council). Amongst the floral tributes were one: "A token of esteem from the local members of the Amalgamated Union of Building Trade Workers", and another, "In affectionate remembrance of our old chairman, Charlie Fisher, from the Cheltenham and District Trades and Labour Council".

GLOSSARY

ammo. ammunition

ANZAC Australian and New Zealand Army Corps

ASC Army Service Corps

AT ?

Blighty England after foreign service

Brag card game

CCS Casualty Clearing Station

CE Chief Engineer

C.O. Commanding Officer

coal-box shell-burst, generally from a heavy gun, causing a cloud of black smoke

comm. trench communication trench

Coy. company

CRE ?

CSM Company Sergeant-Major

Currency All amounts shown are necessarily in terms of the pre-decimal currency of pounds (£), shillings (s) and pence (d). Will's "four shillings" would be our "20p", his "one and fourpence" our "6½p" and his "half a crown" our "12½p"; his final pay of "eight and nine a day" would be our "44p". But one must remember that the purchasing power of the pound would have been vastly different then from what it is now.

DA DRT   Deputy Adjutant – Director of Railway Transport

DCLI   Duke of Cornwall's Light Infantry

destructor   furnace for burning refuse

DS   dressing station

F.A.   Field Ambulance

F.F.   ?

Fritz   German soldier, the Germans

GRO   General Routine Order

GS   General Service

HRS   ?

Jack Johnson   a shell bursting with black smoke, named after negro heavyweight boxing champion – 1908

Jerry   German soldier, the Germans

KRR   King's Royal Rifles

MO   Medical Officer/Orderly

MT   ?

Nap   card game

NCO   non-commissioned officer

OP   Observation Post

O.S.   Overseas Service

Pontoon   card game; support of temporary bridge

QM   Quartermaster

QMS   Quartermaster-Sergeant

RA   Royal Artillery ; Royal Anglesey

RAMC   Royal Army Medical Corps

RE   Royal Engineers

Revet   revetment, strengthening of a trench wall

RGA   Royal Garrison Artillery

ROD   ?

RTO   Railway Transport Officer

SA   Salvation Army

Sapper   This was (and still is) the RE publication
and an attempt has been made to check back
numbers. However, as pseudonyms were used
by contributors and censorship forbade
identification of companies, no trace of Will
Fisher's possible involvement has been found.

shrapnel   steel balls ejected from a shell upon detonation or, more imprecisely, any piece of shell (correctly termed splinters)

scoops   ?

star–lights, star–shells   kind of white light sent up into the air to show enemy's night movements, etc.

SWB   South Wales Borderers

Taube   German two–seater monoplane (Taube is German for 'dove')

(T) Berks   ?

TCL   ?

Terrier   member of British Territorial Force

Tommy   British private soldier (Thomas Atkins)

whizz–bang   a light shell, named from the noise of its approach and detonation

YMCA   Young Men's Christian Association

Any clarification of abbreviations, place-names, etc., would be very much welcomed by the editor.